Phebe

A Real Treasure in the Work of the Lord

Dr. Tom Sexton
Mrs. Nancy Sexton

THE PHEBE FELLOWSHIP

All Scripture quotations are from the Authorized King James Bible.

Tree illustrations by Mrs. Heidi Kriebel.

Printed in the United States of America

This book is dedicated to the ladies
of the Gulf Coast Baptist Church.

"I commend unto you Phebe our sister, which is a
servant of the church which is at Cenchrea: That
ye receive her in the Lord, as becometh saints,
and that ye assist her in whatsoever business she
hath need of you: for she hath been a succourer
of many, and of myself also."

Romans 16:1-2

TABLE OF
CONTENTS

AN INTRODUCTION
TO THE

By Dr. Tom Sexton
Pastor of the Gulf Coast Baptist Church

Romans 16:1, 2, "I commend unto you Phebe our sister, which is a servant of the church which is at Cenchrea: That ye receive her in the Lord, as becometh saints, and that ye assist her in whatsoever business she hath need of you: for she hath been a succourer of many, and of myself also."

God wants women to excel and do something for Him with their lives. The church will never become what God really wants it to become without women doing their part in the work of the Lord.

In two short verses in *Romans* chapter sixteen, we are introduced to this woman, Phebe, one of the great Christians in the New Testament. The Bible says in *Romans 16:1, 2, "I commend unto you Phebe our sister, which is a servant of the church which is at Cenchrea: That ye receive her in the Lord, as becometh saints, and that ye assist her in whatsoever business she hath need of you: for she hath been a succourer of many, and of myself also."*

II Corinthians 10:18 says, *"For not he that commendeth himself is approved, but whom the **Lord** commendeth."* Whom the **Lord** commendeth. I like that! How well it goes with *Romans 16:1, "I commend unto you Phebe."* The **Lord** is commending Phebe, not just an apostle, but the **Lord**. It goes with the spirit of Phebe Fellowship.

Several years ago, I asked the Lord to give me something that would help women, and the Lord gave me a message on Phebe. God really stirred my heart up about it. Every time I read past *Romans 16:1*, this woman's name and life seemed to just leap from the pages and challenge me. I began to think about her life, and I realized she was an unusual woman. God really started stirring my heart about developing something that would strengthen women by taking this woman and highlighting some things out of her life.

Women need encouraging today. There are many things that discourage ladies. I have discovered that there are many women who, every time they try to lift their heads up to do something for God, get pulled down because of a failed marriage, or problems in the home, or maybe a disappointing child. Truly nothing breaks your heart like a disappointing child. Nothing will take the wind out of your sails like a failed home. However, as we examine the Lord's ministry and the Apostle Paul's life and ministry, we find that many of the people that the Lord chose and God used were women who had terrible pasts. Their lives were wrecked and ruined.

Of all the people the Lord used in His earthly ministry, none did He use as much as the woman at the well in *John* chapter four. The only recorded revival under the preaching and teaching ministry of the Lord Jesus took place in Samaria. God used such an unlikely person to reach that city. He chose to use a woman who had been married five times, had given up on it, and now was just living with a guy. The Lord Jesus saved her, turned her life around, empowered her, and used her. If you read *John* chapter four, you will see that this town was rescued, and the Bible says that many of the people in Samaria believed on Him because of the saying of the woman. Yet here is a woman who, if she really had thought about her life, her home, and her children (if she had any), probably would have just thrown in the towel and said, "There is nothing I can do for the Lord."

Again in *Luke* chapter eight, we see that the Lord chose certain women to go with Him on a missions trip, including Mary out of whom went seven devils. Can you imagine what *she* was like before receiving Christ?

The world and sometimes even God's people are hard on women with failed pasts. Men are more often accepted and allowed to reach a higher level of Christian service than women with the same problem past. In the Lord's earthly ministry He chose many women to travel and serve with Him that we would have passed over.

Women with failed pasts can do great things for the Lord. The devil may have gotten the *best* of their lives, but he does not have to get the *rest* of their lives. All through the Bible you see that when the Lord wanted to use people, He chose those who had experienced the grace of God, and they were blessed and used of the Lord.

Do not misunderstand me. I am glad when women have good marriages and wonderful children. We work hard to help them to do that. We work hard to try to strengthen homes and help people raise their children. However, there are many people who would not go very far if their level

9

of Christian service was determined by their success in marriage or children. So the Phebe Fellowship is something that God has given us to help women, to lift them above the things that could pull them down.

We know nothing of Phebe's marriage, if she was married. We know nothing of her family, if she had children. We do not know if she was single, married, or divorced. The Lord did not reveal anything to us about her home life, but we do know that God used her in a mighty way. The Phebe Fellowship is something for women, all women, regardless of whether they are married or single, regardless of whether they have a failed marriage or children that are disappointing.

The Phebe Fellowship is to strengthen women to do something for God with their lives. There are some things that every Christian woman has in common with other Christian women. The Phebe Fellowship "plugs in" to those things. The Bible makes five powerful statements about Phebe. The sixth point about her life we get from the footnote that has been passed down through the centuries. Look at these six things in Phebe's life.

Sister

The Bible says, *"I commend unto you Phebe our **sister**…"* Phebe is a sister. That means there is something special about her. How many of you ladies have a sister? Is she a Christian? Do you have fellowship with her? How many of you ladies have a sister in the Lord that you are close to like a sister? You have a special bond. There is something about a sister in the Lord.

We have taken this statement, *"Phebe our **sister**,"* and we have written some lessons on how to be a sister in the Lord, and how to do some things that every sister should do to strengthen other women. So the first lesson is going to be about just being a good sister.

There are some things that every woman needs from her sisters. When someone joins our church, we want to include them and get them involved in this ministry. We want to get them "plugged in" to what is going on around our church. There is one aspect of the Phebe Fellowship that just strengthens sisters. Sisters need each other.

God has blessed my home. My wife and I have two daughters. All through their childhood they were so close, and they are still close today. I rejoice in that because it is not always that way. There are some things that they got from each other, ways that they strengthened each other. Some of those things I have included in these lessons, things that sisters can do for each other.

Servant

Then the Bible says something else about Phebe, "*which is a servant of the church.*" The Bible does not say she is a servant *in* the church. The Bible says she is a servant *of* the church. That is a whole different statement. If I say, "I am a servant *in* this church," or if I say, "I am a servant *of* this church," you understand there is quite a difference in those statements.

Phebe was a servant of the church. What does it mean to be a servant of the church? Where is a woman's place and role in the ministry? What was it about Phebe's life that made her such a blessing to the church?

She was a servant of the church at Cenchrea. Do you know what that place was like? It was a seaport, a terrible place to live. Can you imagine raising your family in that town? Yet this is where God prepared her for His work. There are some things to learn about being a servant of the church, so the second lesson is on being a servant of the church.

Saint

Then the Bible says, *"That ye receive her in the Lord, **as becometh saints.**"* As becometh saints. What does it mean to be a saint? Better yet, what does *"as becometh saints"* mean? There is a difference in that statement. If I say to you, "You are a saint," you may say, "I do not feel like one." But if you are a Christian, you have been set apart. You are a saint.

But what does *"as becometh"* a saint mean? It implies that progress is being made. She was moving forward in her Christian life, in her walk with God. She was becoming more and more like the Lord Jesus, as becometh a saint. There are some steps in being used of the Lord. Sometimes those steps are easily seen, sometimes not.

The level of your Christian service is determined by the depth of your personal surrender. As becometh a saint has to do with setting yourself apart so God can use you. *You* have to make that decision. The Lord begins to work in your life when you get saved, but how far you go in the work of the Lord is not determined by God, but by you. How much of your life will God have? I think Phebe was a woman who could say, "All that I am, God has." He had all of her. The third lesson has to do with setting ourselves apart for the Lord.

Sent

Then the Bible says that Phebe was sent: *"That ye assist her in whatsoever business she hath need of you."*

God touched this woman, prepared her in Cenchrea, and sent her to Rome. That was not an easy place to live either. They were killing

Christians at Rome. God's people were under tremendous persecution at Rome. The church at Rome was a mission work, and there was something about her life that was going to make a difference on the mission field. She understood what was happening on the front lines. She was the kind of person who could be in touch with the missionary work. The Apostle Paul established the church at Rome, and now Phebe was sent to that place. It was an amazing thing.

The Phebe Fellowship will help develop a heart for missions in our churches. We must do our part in foreign missions and home missions. There ought to be a group of ladies who concentrate on missions and help missionary families who are on the field. Imagine what it is like to have a birthday on a foreign field and not have Grandma come to the birthday party. Some missionaries are working in very difficult areas.

God wanted to encourage the workers in Rome. He wanted to strengthen that church and help them. So He chose this woman, spoke to her, and sent her to Rome. She must have possessed something that was going to be a blessing to those on the foreign field.

The fourth lesson is on how to help and strengthen our missionaries. Some of the things that will be covered are practical things that can involve the entire church.

Succourer

The Bible says Phebe was a sister. She was a servant of the church. The Bible says to receive her as becometh saints. She was sent to Rome. And then the Bible says, *"She hath been a **succourer** of many."*

*"A **succourer** of many."* What does that mean? That is an unusual word in the Bible. I like these Bible words. We do not use many of them today. What does it mean to be a succourer?

When the Lord Jesus succoureth us, it means He strengthens us. The Bible says in *Hebrews 2:18* that when we are tempted, He is able to come to us in the time of temptation and succour us. *"For in that He Himself hath suffered being tempted, He is able to* **succour** *them that are tempted."* Succour means to strengthen. There ought to be someone strengthening people.

The other day, I was trying to go to sleep, and I began to think about some people in the church. I thought about one particular family—I will not tell you who they are—but I remember the first visit I made into their home, and the first visit I made into their home *after* they became Christians. I thought about them, and where they are today, and I began to laugh. They have come a long way.

Who has helped them grow in the Lord? We have helped men, but women have helped women. Women have strengthened other women in the ministry. Women can become a source of strength in a church. Phebe was a succourer of many. The fifth lesson is on strengthening women.

Soul Winner

Then we find the last thing, not from the Bible, but from the footnote in the *Book of Romans.* If you have a Bible that has a footnote at the end of *Romans* chapter sixteen, you will see that it says, "Written to the Romans from Corinthus, and sent by Phebe servant of the church at Cenchrea." This is amazing.

God gave us the *Book of Romans* through the Apostle Paul. Paul rolled it up and put it in Phebe's hand, and Phebe carried the *Book of Romans* to the church at Rome. She carried this powerful book.

We spend a lot of time teaching the "Romans Road" and helping people learn how to take others down the "Romans Road." I would like to use this footnote to show that Phebe was a soul winner. She took the "Romans Road." We want to teach and train ladies on how to be faithful witnesses and tell others about Christ.

I believe these six things are the goal of every Christian woman. These six things are what being a Christian lady is all about:

+ *Be a true sister.*
+ *Be a servant of the church.*
+ *Be as becometh saints.*
+ *Be involved in foreign missions.*
+ *Strengthen others.*
+ *Be a faithful witness.*

What pulls people down is failure, but the Lord is able to lift people above that. The Apostle Paul was able to take women and lift them above that, and they were greatly used of the Lord. The Phebe Fellowship is to help strengthen and encourage women.

In the Phebe Fellowship, we do not talk about the husband and wife relationship. We have other things that do that. We do not talk about how to raise children. The truth of the matter is, everyone has their own opinion about it. (We are all authorities when we have grandchildren!) Your children will grow up, believe it or not, and one day they will leave home. Some people build their lives around their children, and when the children are gone, they have nothing else to live for. Some people build their lives around their marriage. Marriage is important, but some people do not have the greatest marriage in the world. However, they can still do something for God with their lives.

When the Lord Jesus went down to Galilee in *Luke* chapter eight, He called three women, one of whom was married to Herod's steward. Can you imagine what that house was like? Herod was not friendly to Christians. Yet the man who took care of all of his finances had a wife who took off to Galilee with Jesus. I think that is humorous. She said, "I am going down to reach people for God. See you later." Herod was trying to kill the Lord Jesus, and now the Lord Jesus was using Herod's steward's wife to rescue people in Galilee.

There is something greater than what pulls us down. If we can reach higher, we can accomplish something for God with our lives. Phebe discovered the secret of living above the problems of life. She lived on a level that other women can live on. The Phebe Fellowship will help women reach that level.

These lessons were written by me and taught by my dear wife, Nancy, who recorded the Phebe Fellowship. I only wish you could hear her sweet voice as she teaches these lessons.

Women who get a hold of the Phebe Fellowship will discover that it is not just about learning the lessons and getting a certificate; it is about being transformed by these six great truths. The Phebe Fellowship will become a way of life.

A SISTER IN THE LORD

Chapter One

The purpose of the Phebe Fellowship is to provide an opportunity for Christian women to work together in accomplishing the work of the Lord.

In *Romans* chapter sixteen, we are introduced to Phebe. In two short verses we see qualities that every woman who desires to be used of the Lord should possess. Women like Phebe are needed more today than ever before, women who stand in the gap for the Lord Jesus. May the Lord help us to have these qualities in our lives.

First, Phebe was a sister in the Lord. In *Romans 16:1, 2*, the Bible says, *"I commend unto you Phebe our **sister**, which is a servant of the church which is at Cenchrea: That ye receive her in the Lord, as becometh saints, and that ye assist her in whatsoever business she hath need of you: for she hath been a succourer of many, and of myself also."*

*"I commend unto you Phebe our **sister**."* This is a very dear statement about this lady.

One of the special blessings about being a Christian is that we have a wonderful family. We who know Christ as our personal Saviour have a spiritual family, both on earth and in Heaven. *Ephesians 3:15* says, *"Of whom the whole family in heaven and earth is named."*

It is our desire for women who join our church to feel a part and have a sense of belonging, not to feel like outsiders. Therefore, Christian ladies must work at including them and getting them involved in the ministry. If women do not feel at home and welcome they will never reach their full potential in the Lord's work.

There is a bond that all believers have. In *Romans 8:15, 16,* the Bible says, *"For ye have not received the spirit of bondage again to fear; but ye have received the Spirit of adoption, whereby we cry, Abba, Father. The Spirit itself beareth witness with our spirit, that we are the children of God."* This bond is more than friendship. It is the result of the Holy Spirit's work in the believer's life.

What does it really mean to be a sister in the Lord? How can a Christian lady become a better sister? I have taken the word SISTER and made an acrostic to help us see what a true sister in the Lord should be. As we study this lesson, may we become true sisters to each other.

Saved

The first letter in the word sister is *"s"*. *"S"* stands for SAVED. A sister in the Lord is someone who is in the same spiritual family. *John 1:12, 13* says, *"But as many as received Him, to them gave He power to become the sons of God, even to them that believe on His name: Which were born, not of blood, nor of the will of the flesh, nor of the will of man, but of God."*

I was born in Queens, New York, and was raised Catholic. My whole family was Italian Catholic. I was raised in the Catholic church, made my communion and my confirmation, and went to Catholic school in my younger years. I thought I was a good Catholic. Later we moved to Florida because of my sister's health. There I met my husband in high school and shortly after we graduated, we were married. I was a child bride.

My husband's brother, Clarence Sexton, was a Baptist minister. I did not know anything about any other church besides the Catholic church. I knew nothing about Baptists except that my husband's brother was one. He started praying for us, and continued to pray for us for nine years before we got saved.

One evening we attended a church service at Emmanuel Baptist Church because Pastor Riley had asked my brother-in-law to preach there. It was the first time we ever heard him preach. During the whole service my husband held onto the pew so tightly that his knuckles were white. He had his weird-looking sunglasses on - he wore them everywhere - part of his usual attire. But the Lord really spoke to his heart, so that night when we went home, he prayed the sinner's prayer. He waited until we got home of course. He would not go forward in the invitation. I do not think his knuckles could have been pried from the pew!

The next day, I told him he should tell his brother that he had gotten saved. He said, "Do you think he would really want to know?" Can you imagine? I said, "Yes!" We had to get up really early because my husband went to work at six o'clock in the morning, but we drove out to where Clarence was staying with his mom, and Tommy told him about his being saved. His brother said, "That is good." I do not think Clarence really believed that he got saved. My husband said, "Well, I prayed that prayer." He did not really know what to say.

We started attending services at Emmanuel Baptist Church, and the pastor sent some men by our house to talk to my husband about his salvation and about getting baptized. Then they looked at me and asked, "Do you want to be baptized?" I said, "Sure. I will do that." So the next church service we both got baptized.

Soon thereafter, Pastor Riley had a Tuesday morning meeting with Dr. Lee Roberson who spoke on making sure you are saved. He went through the whole plan of salvation. Very few people were there, just a handful, and I was the only one who was lost. Isn't it amazing how the Lord works? I did not realize I was unsaved until Dr. Roberson started talking about nailing down your salvation, and as he was asking questions, I thought, "I am not sure about that." That morning I went forward and got saved.

That is how the Lord first used Dr. Roberson in my life. It still amazes me. Dr. Roberson is such a great man, yet God sent him to that church just so I could get saved. How wonderful! I nailed down my salvation. It is funny how the Lord uses things, because a year after we were saved, we moved to Tennessee and joined Highland Park Baptist Church where Dr. Lee Roberson was pastor.

The Bible says, *"But as many as received Him, to them gave He power to become the sons of God, even to them that believe on His name: Which were born…of God."* Look at the word *"born."* We are born into the family of God when we receive Christ.

If you have children, they were born to you, and there is nothing they can do, no matter how bad, to be *un*born to you. When you are saved, accepting the Lord as your personal Saviour, you are born into the family of God. Once you are born into God's family, He is your heavenly Father. That should help you nail down your salvation right there.

We are born into the family of God when we receive Christ.

We are born into the family of God when we receive Christ. In *John 1:12*, the Bible says, *"But as many as received Him..."* How do we receive Him?

First, we must realize that we are sinners. *"For all have sinned, and come short of the glory of God" (Romans 3:23)*. When we witness to people, we need to remember that they cannot get saved if they do not realize they are lost. They have to realize that they are sinners. A lot of people, surprisingly enough, do not think they are sinners. They really do not think this applies to them. But we are all sinners. We all were born with that sin nature. *"Wherefore, as by one man sin entered into the world, and death by sin; and so death passed upon all men, for that all have sinned" (Romans 5:12)*.

Second, we must believe there is a payment for our sin. *"The wages of sin is death; but the gift of God is eternal life through Jesus Christ our Lord" (Romans 6:23)*. In this world today, we have to pay for everything. Nothing is really free. There is a payment for sin. *"Be not deceived; God is not mocked: for whatsoever a man soweth, that shall he also reap" (Galatians 6:7)*. There is no doubt about that. There is a payment for sin, and the payment is death.

Third, we must believe that the Lord Jesus died for us. *"But God commendeth His love toward us, in that, while we were yet sinners, Christ died for us" (Romans 5:8)*. God sent His precious Son, Jesus, to die in our place on the cross.

Fourth, we must personally pray and receive Christ as our Saviour. Personally. We each personally have to pray the sinner's prayer.

We each personally have to receive Him. It is a personal thing. No one can do it for anyone else.

I saw my husband get saved and thought, "I am glad you are saved—you *need* to be saved!" There was a big change when he got saved. I just seemed to always be the same kind of person. I could relate to *him* being saved. He *needed* it. But me? Yes, I too had to personally pray and receive Christ, just as my husband did.

"That if thou shalt confess with thy mouth the Lord Jesus, and shalt believe in thine heart that God hath raised Him from the dead, thou shalt be saved" (Romans 10:9). "For whosoever shall call upon the name of the Lord shall be saved" (Romans 10:13). If we miss that step, and only get baptized, we are going to miss Heaven. It is a personal thing that we each have to do.

Before we can become true sisters in the Lord, we must each experience the new birth. That is very important, because if we doubt our salvation, we cannot be victorious Christians, and then it is hard to help others. We each need to nail it down. To be true sisters, we must experience the new birth ourselves. In *John 3:7*, the Bible says, *"Marvel not that I said unto thee, Ye must be born again."*

When we receive Christ in repentance and faith we receive the Spirit of adoption.

When we receive Christ in repentance and faith we receive the Spirit of adoption. In *Romans 8: 15, 16* the Bible says, *"For ye have not received the spirit of bondage again to fear; but ye have received the Spirit of adoption, whereby we cry, Abba, Father. The Spirit itself beareth witness with our spirit, that we are the children of God."*

We are placed into the same spiritual family when we are saved.

We are placed into the same spiritual family when we are saved. That means we all have the same Father. We are in the same family, and it is a spiritual family. In *Ephesians 3:15* the Bible says, *"Of whom the whole family in heaven and earth is named."* Verses *17* through *19* say, *"That Christ may dwell in your hearts by faith; that ye, being rooted and grounded in love, May be able to comprehend with all saints what is the breadth, and length, and depth, and height; And to know the love of Christ, which passeth knowledge, that ye might be filled with all the fulness of God."*

It takes a while to feel like a part of the family. When people get saved and join a church family, it takes a while to feel at home. Many times people are not comfortable, especially coming in new. We remember how that feels. We were all new once. I do not like to come into new situations. I like to be comfortable. I like to know people. It takes a while to feel a part of the family.

We need to welcome new women into our church family. That is one of the reasons the Lord gave us the Phebe Fellowship. This is a church family and we need to welcome new ladies. If we do not do our part, they will never feel a part. We have to do our part for new ladies to feel a part of this church family.

How do we make people feel welcome? We need to extend ourselves and be friendly. We need to greet visitors and learn their names. When they come in the door, we should introduce ourselves. Say, "Hi! I am Nancy Sexton." That is not too hard, ladies. I know. I am shy myself. Ask them their name and repeat it. "It is very nice to meet you, Lisa. I am so glad you are here!"

Then show visitors around. In our church we know where everything is, but new people do not. Make a map of where all the Sunday school classes are. If visitors have children, show them where their children go. Do not just tell them; go with them and help them. Introduce them to other people and especially to the pastor.

We also need to sit with ladies who come alone. No one likes to come in and sit alone. That is hard for a lady to do. The ladies who are a part of the Phebe Fellowship should be the welcome wagon in our churches.

Phebe was saved. A sister in the Lord is not only Saved, but she is also someone with Influence.

Influence

How important is influence? Can we make a difference in the lives of other ladies and *not* have influence? A sister in the Lord is someone who has influence over the lives of others.

Romans 14:7 says, *"For none of us liveth to himself, and no man dieth to himself."* That is so true. This is contrary to the world's thinking. I remember when I was lost and my friends told me, "Whatever you do, it is no one's business. It is your life. Do what you want." But that is not true at all. What we do affects everyone.

I know a woman who had a lot of problems and caused her whole family much heartache. Thank God she is saved today and doing very well, but it took many years and affected her family so much. She used to say, "It is no one's business what I do." I thought, "You think so? Look at your mother. What you are doing is killing her."

What we do affects others whether we like it or not. All of us have influence. People are watching us. We affect people. If we get up in the morning in a bad mood, who does it affect? Everyone who comes in contact with us. If we get up in the morning in a great mood, that also affects people. It is so true that we have influence, either good or bad.

We build our influence by doing two things.

First, we must love and serve the Lord. *Philippians 1:21* says, *"For to me to live is Christ, and to die is gain."* *Matthew 22:37* and *38* say, *"...Thou shalt love the Lord thy God with all thy heart, and with all thy soul, and with all thy mind. This is the first and great commandment."*

We need to love the Lord and not the world. *I John 2:15* says, *"Love not the world, neither the things that are in the world..."* We live in this world and we have to put up with a lot of worldly things, but we do not have to love the things of this world. We should keep our distance from worldly things because they affect our influence. We cannot hang around the wrong friends and wrong things and not expect our influence to be hurt.

Second, we must love others more than ourselves. We must be willing to live for others. *Philippians 2:20* and *21* say, *"For I have no man likeminded, who will naturally care for your state. For all seek their own, not the things which are Jesus Christ's."* In *Matthew 22:39* Jesus says, *"And the second is like unto it, Thou shalt love thy neighbour as thyself."* We need to love others more than ourselves.

The world teaches us to love ourselves before we can love others. How many times have we heard that one? "You have to love yourself before you can love others." God's Word teaches that loving ourselves is something we should not do.

People are born loving themselves. I have granddaughters, and people tell them how pretty they are. Just ask Rachel and she will tell you, "Oh, I am so pretty. I look pretty in this dress." She is funny.

We are taught to love ourselves. As children our mothers kept telling us how pretty we were, our pretty dresses, our pretty hair. If we ate our carrots, we would have pretty eyes. We are taught to love ourselves, and in one sense it is important to love and take care of ourselves. We only have one body to serve the Lord with, and we need to take care of it.

However, we have to be taught to love others. Loving others does not come naturally.

Everyone lives in either *Philippians 1:21* or *Philippians 2:21*. *Philippians 1:21* says, *"For to me to live is Christ, and to die is gain."* *Philippians 2:21* says, *"For all seek their own, not the things which are Jesus Christ's."* We are in one place or the other. We are either loving Christ and others, or we are loving ourselves.

II Timothy 3:2 says, *"For men shall be lovers of their own selves…"* This is one of the signs of the last days. We all know people like that, people in love with themselves, stuck on themselves. That is not how the Bible teaches Christians to be.

We build our influence by loving God and living for others. That means we do not think of ourselves first, and we do not put ourselves first. *I Corinthians 8:3* says, *"But if any man love God, the same is known of him."* Without influence, we simply cannot be very helpful to others.

Someone said the way to spell joy is

Jesus first

Others second

Yourself last

Jesus first, others second, and ourselves last. Do we have joy?

Those who love the Lord and live for others are Christians with great influence. If we want to be Christians with great influence, we have to love and serve the Lord, and be willing to live for others.

We love those who have a positive influence on our lives.

We love those who have a positive influence on our lives. *Philippians 1:3* and *7* say, *"I thank my God upon every remembrance of you…because I have you in my heart…"* I have several ladies in my life that I thank God for.

Mrs. Lee Roberson had such an influence in my life as a new Christian. I used to watch her, and what encouraged me so much about her is that, though she was a very quiet and shy lady, she supported and helped her husband *and* worked in the nursery. She was in charge of the whole nursery, which was very large at Highland Park Baptist Church with hundreds of children, sometimes as many as four hundred on Sunday mornings. She headed up the nursery and made sure everything ran right. I thought, "I can do that."

I almost had a heart attack when my husband was called to preach, because I thought, "*I* have to be a *pastor's* wife?" I too am very shy, but I looked at Mrs. Roberson, and she helped me so much to get over that shock. I thought, "I can be like her. I can find something to do without being in the limelight."

My sister-in-law, Evelyn Sexton, taught me how to cook. I was born in New York, and all we ate was spaghetti and Italian dishes, so Evelyn taught me how to make cornbread and pinto beans and all the good stuff,

and better than that too. She started a cooking class with me, and I enjoyed it so much. She was such a blessing in my life. She helped me with so many things, not just cooking. She was a good example of a pastor's wife to me. I would watch her and try to glean from her life.

My husband and I knew a lady named Mrs. Paschal whose husband was the chairman of the deacons at the church where we were students. Every Christmas, she brought me a big shirt-box of cookies and goodies. That was such a blessing to me. She did not have to do that. She did not have to extend herself like that to others.

Another lady, Mrs. Jean Smith, would have us over to her home for missionary meetings. Here we were, just students. There were many church members and students that went there. But Mrs. Smith would extend herself and her home. At her front entrance, she had a beautiful portrait of her daughter in her wedding dress. I did the same for both of my girls, which I have enjoyed so much. There were so many things I learned. I watched how she set the table and how she arranged things.

We can learn by going to people's homes. We can learn so much by watching people. We all have people in our lives that we look up to. We learn things when we sit back and watch, but we do not need to *keep* sitting back. *We* need to be the doers. *We* need to extend ourselves. *We* need to have great influence. The only way to do that is to live for others.

There are two questions that we should consider:

1. Who do we have in our hearts?

2. Who has us in their hearts?

Think about these questions. Who has invested their lives in us? In whom are we investing our lives? At the end of our lives, how will we be remembered? Will we continue to live in the hearts of others? We have all been to funerals. In some of them the family and friends talk about the person, and we think, "What a great person." But what will people say about us? Do people have us in their hearts? Do we have people in our hearts?

When the name Phebe was mentioned, the hearts of others were stirred. I pray that we would all learn how to be better Christians and extend ourselves to others. I pray that we would all grow and mature and be better servants for the Lord, and that He would teach us all great things.

Phebe was a sister in the Lord. She was Saved, and she had Influence.

Strengthens

A sister in the Lord is someone who strengthens others. *Proverbs 27:17* says, *"Iron sharpeneth iron; so a man sharpeneth the countenance of his friend."* We do not sharpen iron by hitting it. We sharpen it by crossing it. When we sharpen a knife, we do not hit it, we draw it across another blade. That is what the Bible means when it says, *"Iron sharpeneth iron."* Our lives crossing the lives of others sharpen them.

When iron is sharpened, there is friction. We can even see sparks sometimes if we look closely. When people are sharpened, there will be some friction and sparks. Nothing ever runs perfectly smoothly. There will always be friction and sparks. When we sharpen others, it is not always easy, but we do need to strengthen others.

I Samuel 23:16 says, *"And Jonathan Saul's son arose, and went to David into the wood, and **strengthened his hand in God**."* We have all been strengthened or weakened by people we know. We need to think about what kind of people *we* are. Do we strengthen or weaken people?

We strengthen others when we stand with them and support them in their right decisions.

Joshua 24:15 says, *"And if it seem evil unto you to serve the LORD,* **choose** *you this day whom ye will serve…As for me and my house, we will serve the LORD."* What a great verse. The key word here is "choose." Life is filled with choices.

The quality of our lives is determined by the quality of decisions we make. We have to remember that. Many people wonder, "Why is this happening to me? Why did God let this happen to me?" We cannot blame the Lord for everything. That is like saying, "The devil made me do it." That is not true. Most of the messes we get in are because of bad decisions we have made, and we have all made bad decisions. The decisions that we make constitute our lives.

How can we know if we are making the right decisions? When facing decisions, we can ask ourselves the following questions:

Does it please the Lord? *John 8:29* says, *"…For I do always those things that please Him."*

Rivers are always interesting to me. I love to go up in the mountains of Tennessee and see those rivers. Did you know that rivers take the course of least resistance? Rivers are never perfectly straight. They are always crooked. People who take the course of least resistance in life will look back and see that their lives have turned time and time again. But *we* do not want to "go with the flow" through our lives as Christians. We want to make quality decisions. We need to stop and think about the decisions we are making. Does it please the Lord? Pleasing the Lord is the highest goal of a Christian's life. That is the most important question. Does it please the Lord?

Pleasing the Lord is the highest goal of a Christian's life.

Can we put our hearts in it? *Colossians 3:17* says, *"And whatsoever ye do in word or deed, do all in the name of the Lord Jesus, giving thanks to God and the Father by Him."* Verse *23* says, *"And whatsoever ye do, do it heartily, as to the Lord, and not unto men."* We have to be careful to consider why we are doing the things we do. Are we doing them for man's praise? That is going to get old, ladies. We have to be doing them for the Lord. If we are doing them for the Lord, we probably will not stress ourselves out so much. We will have it all in perspective. The key is to put our hearts in it. There are so many things that are killing us because our hearts are not in it. Can we put our hearts in it?

The Lord will increase our desire when it is His will. *Psalm 37:4* says, *"Delight thyself also in the LORD; and He shall give thee the desires of thine heart."* That is encouraging. God is not going to have us do something that we hate. He will definitely increase our desire. When God encourages our hearts, it increases our desire. We will know it is His will. Desire is the motor that drives the Christian life.

What would other Christians think of it? *Romans 14:7* says, *"For none of us liveth to himself, and no man dieth to himself."*

First, we should be concerned about what those who have helped us think about our decision. Once someone has invested their life in us we should always remember them and their influence. *Hebrews 13:7* says,

"Remember them which have the rule over you, who have spoken unto you the Word of God: whose faith follow, considering the end of their conversation."

Hebrews 13:17 tells us, *"Obey them that have the rule over you, and submit yourselves: for they watch for your souls, as they that must give account, that they may do it with joy, and not with grief: for that is unprofitable for you."* For this reason we honor our spiritual leaders and their testimonies and walk with Christ.

Paul said that the believers at Thessalonica were his crown of rejoicing in *I Thessalonians 2:19: "For what is our hope, or joy, or crown of rejoicing? Are not even ye in the presence of our Lord Jesus Christ at His coming?"* We each are someone's crown of rejoicing. All those who have helped us become what we are should be rejoicing over our lives, work, and testimonies.

Second, we should consider ladies we are trying to help when we make decisions. Many new Christians and weaker Christians will be affected by our decisions. We learn from God's Word that sometimes even good things must be avoided for weaker Christians or babes in Christ. *"Wherefore, if meat make my brother to offend, I will eat no flesh while the world standeth, lest I make my brother to offend" (I Corinthians 8:13).*

Ladies who understand the importance of their influence will always consider how their lives affect others. It is true that no one lives and dies without having influence on someone. *Romans 14:7* says, *"For none of us liveth to himself, and no man dieth to himself."*

Do we have any doubt about it? *Romans 14:23* says, *"And he that doubteth is damned if he eat, because he eateth not of faith: for whatsoever is not of faith is sin."*

If we have doubt, that is a "no" answer from God. If there is any doubt, do not do it. Doubt does not mean fear. Doubt means there is a question about it.

When we ask ourselves these things, and we come to the "doubt" question above, the answer should become clearer. But if we still have so much doubt and wonder if we should do it, then we better stop and step back and really pray about it. That hesitation could be the Lord saying no.

A God-blessed life is the result of making right decisions. The quality of our lives is determined by the quality of the decisions we make.

The quality of our lives is determined by the quality of the decisions we make.

If we want ladies to stand with us and support us in our decisions, then we must be able to answer these four questions. On the other hand, if we are going to help strengthen others, we need to make sure we are strengthening them to do the right things. When our friends come to us for counsel, we need to go through these questions to ensure we are steering them in the right way.

We strengthen others when we help them to be their best for the Lord.

"Iron sharpeneth iron" means to sharpen up. We have all been strengthened by someone, and we need to strengthen others.

There *is* a Christian culture. Jesus said, *"Ye are the light of the world…" (Matthew 5:14)*. There are only two kinds of people, saved and unsaved. There should be a noticeable difference between saved people and lost people. The Lord Jesus said that His followers are children of light. *I Thessalonians 5:5* says, *"Ye are all the children of light, and the children of the day: we are not of the night, nor of darkness."* There is a difference between the culture of the children of light and the culture of the children of darkness. In the Christian culture, all of our decisions should be made in the light of God's Word.

A sister in the Lord is Saved. She has Influence over the lives of others. She Strengthens others by standing with them and supporting them in their right decisions. A sister is also someone who is Trustworthy.

Trustworthy

A sister is trustworthy. A sister in the Lord is a friend that can be trusted with precious things. *Proverbs 17:17* says, *"A friend loveth at all times…"* *Proverbs 27:6* says, *"Faithful are the wounds of a friend…"* *Proverbs 27:9* says, *"Ointment and perfume rejoice the heart: so doth the sweetness of a man's friend by hearty counsel."* *Psalm 62:8* says, *"Trust in Him at all times; ye people, pour out your heart before Him: God is a refuge for us."*

A true friend is someone that you can trust.

True friends can be trusted because they love us and desire God's best for us. When we have the right kind of friends, we do not have any problems trusting them. *Psalm 62:8* says, *"Trust in Him at all times…"*

A true friend is someone to whom you can pour out your heart.

Everyone needs someone to talk to. *Psalm 62:8* says, *"...pour out your heart before Him..."* We just need to be careful, ladies, of what we say to people. People are human beings. We have that human nature.

The Bible says to confess our faults, not our sins, and there is a big difference between them. *"Confess your faults one to another, and pray one for another, that ye may be healed. The effectual fervent prayer of a righteous man availeth much" (James 5:16).*

We need to be careful about pouring our hearts out to others. We can always pour our hearts out to the Lord. We can tell Him anything we want to, and He is the best friend we will ever have. There are *some* things we need to just pray about.

A true friend will comfort you through the storms of life.

Sometimes God does not remove the storms because He wants us to stand strong in them. Sometimes storms help keep us straight. When we have problems and trials and troubles, God does not always remove them. We pray, "Oh, Lord, please take this away." But many times, He does not want to remove them. He has allowed them for a reason. Even though we cannot figure it out, God knows. He wants us to stand strong, and He will give us strength. When the storm is over, we are stronger and we know the Lord has helped us through it. We grow as Christians through trials and testings. *"...God is a refuge for us."* True friends will comfort us and be there for us through those storms.

A sister in the Lord should be someone you can trust with the hurt in your life. I have heard many people say, "I do not have a friend like that. I wish I did." *Proverbs 18:24* says, *"A man that hath friends must shew himself friendly: and there is a friend that sticketh closer than a brother."* I am a shy person. I know it is harder for some people to be friendly. But if we want friends, we are going to have to extend ourselves and show ourselves friendly.

Encourages

A sister in the Lord also knows how to encourage people. She is an encourager. *Hebrew 3:13* says, *"But exhort one another daily, while it is called To day; lest any of you be hardened through the deceitfulness of sin."*

We encourage others by being faithful to church.

Hebrews 10:24 and *25* say, *"And let us consider one another to provoke unto love and to good works: Not forsaking the assembling of ourselves together, as the manner of some is; but exhorting one another: and so much the more, as ye see the day approaching."* That is not just for pastors and leaders and workers. It is for everyone. It is for new Christians, too.

Everyone needs to be faithful because people are looking at our lives. If people see us being faithful they will be encouraged to be faithful too. We need to be in our places. That is so important. When someone is missing from their place, we can really see that they are not there. It is a definite, obvious thing. People are watching us so we need to be in our places. We need to be faithful to the Lord and faithful to church.

I like *II Corinthians 3:2* which says, *"Ye are our epistle written in our hearts, known and read of all men."* People are watching us, so let us be faithful.

When people miss church they become discouraged. The more services people miss, the more they feel embarrassed. I have been talking to a lady, trying to get her to come back to church, but she is so embarrassed because she has missed so many times. Once people start missing, it gets easier and easier to miss more, and harder and harder to come back.

We need to be faithful, and every time we come to church we need to be encouragers. We never know what people are going through.

We encourage others by the things we say.

Proverbs 16:24 says, *"Pleasant words are as an honeycomb, sweet to the soul, and health to the bones."*

We should speak to and encourage others. Pastor always says a pat on the back and "That a girl!" goes a long way. *Proverbs 15:23* says, *"...A word spoken in due season, how good is it!"*

There is a time to talk and a time to listen. In *Job 2:13*, Job had comforters. *"So they sat down with him upon the ground seven days and seven nights, and none spake a word unto him: for they saw that his grief was very great."* People had come to comfort Job, and they *were* a real comfort to him, until they opened their mouths! Then they discouraged him. Instead of being *en*couragers, they became *dis*couragers. It would have been better for them to just go home and not say a word. Job knew that they were his friends and that they loved him, until they opened their mouths.

When we talk to people and try to encourage them, we need to be very sensitive. Sometimes we just need to listen; we do not always need to talk. We always get in trouble with those little things in our mouths called our tongues! Learn how to speak encouraging words to others.

We should write encouraging notes. *Proverbs 12:25* says, *"Heaviness in the heart of man maketh it stoop: but a good word maketh it glad."* Take the time to write a note or speak to someone daily. I received a precious note this week about the Phebe Fellowship, and I really appreciate it. It was so encouraging to me. We need to take time to do such things. We are all so busy, but we all need to stop and take time.

We can make phone calls. Many of us have cell phones in our cars now. Let us use them for the Lord! We should call people that we have missed and take the time to encourage someone every day.

Those who have encouraged us over the years are very dear to us. My memory fails me sometimes, but I can always remember encouraging words. We all can. It is the responsibility of every Christian to encourage someone every day. *Hebrews 3:13* says, *"But exhort one another **daily**…"*

It is the responsibility of every Christian to encourage someone every day.

II Corinthians 1:4 says, *"Who comforteth us in all our tribulation, that we may be able to comfort them which are in any trouble, by the comfort wherewith we ourselves are comforted of God."* Through the trials and troubles we have gone through, we have learned how to be comforted and how to comfort others. I think that is one of the reasons that we go through troubles. It is to teach us how to help others.

There are so many things that I have gone through personally in my life. When we were in college, I prayed to have another child. My husband and I thought that would be a wonderful thing, to have a baby after we were saved. God answered my prayer in a strange way. I did become pregnant, but I had a tubular pregnancy that ruptured, and I had to have three surgeries. I thought, "Lord, why didn't You just say no?" My whole life changed, and I was only twenty-seven years old.

I wondered why I had to go through that, but I learned so many things. Since then, I have had so many ladies come to me with trials and heartaches, and I have shared what I learned through that. Now I know why the Lord allowed me to go through that: so I could encourage others.

Sometimes we go through things that are horrible at the time, but God gets us through and makes us stronger people. Someday, God will send someone our way who is going through the same kind of thing that we can encourage, and that makes it better and softens the blow. We need to be encouragers to others.

Let us take time every day to encourage others. Phebe was such an encourager.

Rejoices

A sister in the Lord is also someone with whom we can rejoice. The Christian life is a life of rejoicing. *I Thessalonians 5:18* says, *"In every thing give thanks: for this is the will of God in Christ Jesus concerning you."*

Proverbs 17:22 says, *"A merry heart doeth good like a medicine…"* I love that verse. It is so true. I have learned how to laugh at myself. No one else may think I am funny, but I do not care. If I laugh at myself, it helps me. If you are nervous, laugh. The Lord has taught me to do that. So if I start giggling, you will know, I am nervous or feeling silly. In our Sunday school class we have a lot of fun; we laugh a lot. When you do something stupid, laugh at yourself.

When we hear someone else laughing, it is so encouraging. It is catching. It makes other people laugh. That is one of the things I like about my husband. He has always been a clown from day one. I was always quiet and shy, so we go together. Opposites do attract. He finds humor in everything.

My husband tells the story of one time when we were in church, shortly after we got saved, and he laughed out loud. He was hysterical. It was while everyone else was praying! I was so humiliated. I was so mad at him. I said, "We will never be able to go back to that church. You have ruined it. We just got saved and look at what you have done." I was so upset with him, because he had made *me* laugh too! Of course, that was my fault. Why should I blame him? But when *he* started laughing, he got *me* laughing, and I could not stop! We were *both* hysterical. It was so stupid.

Learn to laugh at yourself. Before, I used to be mortified if something happened. I would be embarrassed and never want to show my face again. That is not the way to be, because it makes us go deeper and further into our shells. So I have learned to laugh at myself. Everybody else just laughs. So if something funny happens, people laugh, and it is over. I do not know why we get so embarrassed and humiliated. Just laugh about it and go on. And if we watch, it will happen to somebody else! I think that is part of rejoicing and having a merry heart. It is a very catching thing, and it is like a good medicine.

Some people can only rejoice when things are going well. That *is* a good time to rejoice. But when we cannot see the big picture, and things start going badly, we still need to rejoice anyway. We can know that God is in charge of our lives, and He is in control, and He knows what is coming up next. We need to be thankful and have a merry heart.

II Corinthians 4:17 says, *"For our light affliction, which is but for a moment, worketh for us a far more exceeding and eternal weight of glory."* Notice the phrase, *"light affliction."* Sometimes we feel like we have the weight of the world on our shoulders. When we feel that way, it is our fault. We are not giving our affliction to the Lord. We are not praying. We should ask the Lord to let us join the Merry Heart Club.

The Merry Heart Club believes three things according to II Corinthians 4:17.

"For our light affliction, which is but for a moment, worketh for us a far more exceeding and eternal weight of glory."

No problem is bigger than the Lord Jesus.
"Our light affliction..."

When we put our problems at the feet of Jesus, we see how tiny they are. Sometimes we make mountains out of molehills. We need to keep it all in perspective. There is no problem that is larger than the Lord Jesus.

No trouble lasts forever.
"...which is but for a moment..."

That is encouraging. Everyone has problems whether they are saved or unsaved. *Job 14:1* says, *"Man that is born of a woman is of few days, and full of trouble."* We are all born of woman, and we are all full of trouble, but no problem lasts forever. There is always light at the end of

the tunnel. The only way to avoid trouble is not to be born. Really, ladies, everyone has problems and troubles. If we will keep them all in perspective, we will be okay.

A great truth for troubled lives is *"It came to pass."* Throughout the Bible, God says, *"And it came to pass..."* All our troubles will one day pass. When trouble comes, where do we run? That is the most important thing. We need to run to the Lord.

Everything that God allows to come into our lives can help make us more like the Lord Jesus.

"...worketh for us a far more exceeding and eternal weight of glory."

Romans 8:28 is a great verse too. *"And we know that all things work together for good to them that love God, to them who are the called according to His purpose."* The Bible says, *"And we **know**..."*

When I lead people to the Lord, I go through the verse, *"For whosoever shall call upon the name of the Lord shall be saved" (Romans 10:13).* Then I ask, "Is God a liar? Does God lie? What does He say? If Joan calls upon the name of the Lord she shall be saved." The Bible is true. When God says, *"And we **know**..."*, we can **know**. We know, ladies, that all things work together for our good. We have to believe that. We cannot see the whole picture, but God can. And He made us, so He knows what is best for us. We have to trust that. *Romans 8:28* is a great verse.

Jacob said in *Genesis 42:36, "...All these things are against me."* Paul said in *Romans 8:28*, "All things are for me." Outlook often determines outcome.

The Merry Heart Club does not quit because of trouble. Just because problems come along, we do not need to quit! Phebe was without a doubt a woman who learned how to rejoice in everything. Anyone rejoicing in the time of trouble gets attention. When we have things go wrong, and we laugh at ourselves, people pay attention. If we start crying, we get attention too. But let us get the *right* attention.

People always are amazed at how Christians handle things. I have heard many people comment about how Christians go through trials and still rejoice in the Lord. God helps us because He gets honor and glory in those hard times when we rejoice. If we rejoice in the real hard troubles that we go through, the Lord gets the honor and glory, and people notice that in us. *Nehemiah 8:10* says, *"...The joy of the LORD is your strength."*

In conclusion, to be the kind of sister in the Lord that makes a difference in the lives of others, we must:

Know Christ as Saviour.	**S**AVED
Build our influence.	**I**NFLUENCE
Strengthen others.	**S**TRENGTHENS
Be trustworthy.	**T**RUSTWORTHY
Encourage others.	**E**NCOURAGES
Rejoice in everything.	**R**EJOICES

If we want to be true sisters like Phebe, we need to study these lessons and let the Lord help us grow to be stronger Christians. I pray the Lord will drive these things home in our hearts, and guide us to ladies in our church who need us, and who are going through difficulties. I pray that we will be Phebes, sisters in the Lord, and be what He wants us to be.

A SERVANT OF THE CHURCH

Chapter Two

Romans 16:1, 2, "I commend unto you Phebe our sister, which is a servant of the church which is at Cenchrea: That ye receive her in the Lord, as becometh saints, and that ye assist her in whatsoever business she hath need of you: for she hath been a succourer of many, and of myself also."

In our first lesson, we learned that Phebe was a sister. Now we see that she was a servant. She knew that the purpose of the Christian life is to be a servant. Most people wonder and search trying to find out what life is all about, but Phebe knew. As a Christian, her purpose was to be a servant of the Lord. We all need to be servants of the Lord.

When the Lord spoke of the death of Moses, one of the greatest leaders who ever lived, He said, *"Moses My servant is dead" (Joshua 1:2).* Can you imagine the Lord saying, "Nancy My servant…"? Put *your* name in place of Moses' name. What a compliment for the Lord to call Moses His servant. What a great example Moses set for us.

When my husband and I were new Christians, Dr. Lee Roberson was our "Moses." That is why we talk about him so much. He is the best Christian we have ever known. He is a humble and dedicated man, truly a servant of the Lord. We are so thankful to the Lord that we were able to be under his ministry and learn all the things we did from him.

We all need to be known as servants. The Apostle Paul tells us of Christ being a servant. In *Philippians 2:7* the Bible says, *"But made Himself of no reputation, and took upon Him the form of a servant..."* In a day when so many desire to be served, it is refreshing to hear of those who are willing to be servants.

One of the things that made Phebe such a great lady was that she was a servant. She was willing to be a servant of the church. She had a heart to help people.

My husband and I ate out the other night and had a waitress who did not want to serve us. My husband would say, "Excuse me, ma'am, may I have...?" And she would say, "Can't you see that I only have two hands?" We were so surprised. Every time he said anything, she would respond that way. Of course, most waitresses are so loving and attentive. They will ask throughout the meal, "Is there anything I can get for you?" They are such blessings because they are willing to serve.

We need to be servants. How do we act toward other people? Do they hate to see us coming? Do we act like we need to be served? We should be servants. *II Corinthians 4:5* says, *"For we preach not ourselves, but Christ Jesus the Lord; and ourselves your servants for Jesus' sake."* Are we willing to be servants? How we feel toward those who treat us like servants reveals whether or not we have a servant's heart.

The church needs servants. Christian ladies who are willing to find their place of service can make a difference in the lives of people. One of our church mottoes is "Making A Difference In The Lives Of People" from *Jude 22, "...Some have compassion, making a difference."* Every serious-minded Christian should have a place of service in the local church. There is a job for everyone. There should be no unemployment in the Lord's work. As we study this lesson may we all find our place of service.

Examples of Women in the Work of the Lord

Many ladies ask, "What can I do as a woman?" Many ladies think there is no place of service for them. The Bible is full of examples of women in the work of the Lord.

Women served with the Lord Jesus in His earthly ministry.

The Lord chose certain women to aid and assist in His earthly ministry. What a privilege these women had to work with the Lord Jesus. Imagine serving with the Lord, following Him around, and being His servant for even one day. Imagine the opportunity. These ladies got to be with the Lord Jesus Christ and serve Him. Think about the miracles they saw and everything they experienced first-hand.

Luke 8:1-3 says, *"And it came to pass afterward, that He went throughout every city and village, preaching and shewing the glad tidings of the kingdom of God: and the twelve were with Him, And* ***certain women****, which had been healed of evil spirits and infirmities,*

Mary called Magdalene, out of whom went seven devils, And Joanna the wife of Chuza Herod's steward, and Susanna, and many others, which ministered unto Him of their substance." The Lord took these *"certain women"* traveling with Him.

If the Lord gave *us* the job of choosing certain women in this church to travel with Him, whom would *we* choose? These women the Lord chose had problems. They *really* had problems! One of them had several devils in her before she got saved. Another one was the wife of Herod's steward. We would suspect she was a traitor. It is interesting how the Lord uses people. He does not always use whom we would think.

The Lord used these *"certain women."* He did not use perfect women who had perfect homes and perfect marriages and perfect children and perfect lives. There is no such thing. He chose women who had problems. That is encouraging! The Lord uses anyone who is willing. What kind of women did the Lord Jesus choose?

He chose women who knew Him as their personal Saviour. *Luke 8:2* says, *"…which had been healed of evil spirits and infirmities…"* These women knew Him as their personal Saviour. They knew beyond any doubt. *We* must know beyond any doubt.

The Bible says in *I John 5:13, "These things have I written unto you that believe on the name of the Son of God; that ye may **know** that ye have eternal life, and that ye may believe on the name of the Son of God."* I like a "know-so" salvation. Once we know the Lord as Saviour, we can stand on His promises and believe on Him to do something in our lives for Him. God can bless and use us when we have assurance of our salvation.

I John 2:3 says, *"And hereby we do **know** that we **know** Him, if we keep His commandments."* We can know in our hearts that we know the Lord because we keep His commandments. We have a desire in our hearts to yield our lives to the Lord and to do what He has commanded us to do.

In *I John 3:14* the Bible says, *"We **know** that we have passed from death unto life, because we love the brethren…"* We can know that we are saved when we have a love in our hearts for God's people.

The Bible says in *I John 4:13, "Hereby **know** we that we dwell in Him, and He in us, because He hath given us of His Spirit."* Another way that we can know that we know Him is that the Holy Spirit indwells, convicts, and guides our lives.

Others should know that we know Christ as Saviour. The Bible says in *John 13:35, "By this shall all men **know** that ye are My disciples, if ye have love one to another."*

We must tell people that *they* can receive the Lord Jesus Christ as *their* personal Saviour. *I John 4:14* says, *"And we have seen and do testify that the Father sent the Son to be the Saviour of the world."*

He chose women who had a heart for the ministry. That is important. *Luke 8:3* says that these were women *"…which ministered unto Him of their substance."* They were women who rejoiced over what the Lord was doing, and supported it with their substance. That means they supported it with what they had: their treasure, their time, and their talents.

To have a heart for the ministry means to have a heart for people. We can go through the motions but if we do not have a heart for people, a heart for the ministry, our service will become a great chore. It will grow old quickly. A personal test to see if we are servants is to gauge how we feel in our hearts toward people who treat us like servants.

I do not know why, but every time my daughters and I go shopping, someone stops me to ask me a question about the store, and I have to tell them, "I don't work here." Then I ask my daughters, "Do I look like I work here?"

Mandy and I were looking for wallpaper at the Home Depot, and Mandy was flipping through the books. She used to work at a wallpaper store and she is really good at decorating. A lady came up to her and started talking to her as if she worked there. Mandy said, "I don't work here, but what do you need? I will try to help you find it." I thought, "That is an illustration of a servant's heart."

Being a servant is having a willing heart, thinking of other people, putting others before self. The Lord is looking for women who know Him and have a willing heart to serve others.

Women had a part in the first church prayer meeting.

Women had a part in the first church prayer meeting. We always hear about men serving in the church, but women did too. *Acts 1:14* says, *"These all continued with one accord in prayer and supplication,* **with the women**, *and Mary the mother of Jesus, and with His brethren."* They were all in one accord in prayer and supplication *"with the women."* The women were right there with them. Even though it was a men's prayer meeting, Mary was there, and so were other women.

What have we waited on the Lord for? What have we prayed for and waited to see happen? What prayers have we seen answered? We have prayer meetings, and we take prayer requests and pray, but we need to make it real. We each need to have a prayer list, and write down not just requests, but also answers to prayer. It is a blessing to look at our prayer lists and see the prayers God has already answered. We are encouraged to know that He has answered our prayers before, and this helps us to wait.

Many promises are for those who wait. *Isaiah 40:31* says, *"But they that wait upon the LORD shall renew their strength; they shall mount up with wings as eagles; they shall run, and not be weary; and they shall walk, and not faint."*

Waiting on the Lord is one of the most difficult things to do in the Christian life. Sometimes it is difficult to wait on the Lord because of the pressure that others put on us. *Psalm 25:3* says, *"Yea, let none that wait on Thee be ashamed: let them be ashamed which transgress without cause."*

Acts 1:14 says, *"These all continued with* **one accord** *in prayer and supplication, with the women..."* The prayers of godly women who were in one accord made a difference. There is power in prayer, especially when godly women get together and pray. The Bible says where two or more are gathered together in His name, He will answer prayer. *"Again I say unto you, That if two of you shall agree on earth as touching any thing that they shall ask, it shall be done for them of My Father which is in heaven. For where two or three are gathered together in My name, there am I in the midst of them" (Matthew 18:19, 20).* Prayer really makes a difference. Women can be servants of the church by praying in one accord.

Women played an important role in the life and ministry of the Apostle Paul.

Philippians 4:3 says, *"And I intreat thee also, true yokefellow, help those women which laboured with me in the gospel..."* The gospel ministry is serving *with* Christ not just *for* Christ. These women understood the work of the Lord and labored with the Apostle Paul in

the gospel. Women who understand the work of the Lord are valuable to the cause of Christ.

The Lord Jesus had certain people that we call the "inner circle" that traveled with Him as He ministered to people. The Apostle Paul also had people who traveled with him as he blazed a trail for Christ. Many of the inner circle who traveled with Christ and Paul were ladies who had been transformed by the gospel and who understood the work of the Lord.

Some people do not understand when leaders have to make decisions, or when things have to be done a certain way. If godly women understand the work of the Lord, they will understand why things have to be done the way they are. Churches have problems usually because of *mis*understandings. We need to pray for understanding.

There were many women who labored with Paul in the gospel and one of them was Phebe. These women labored *with* him, not *for* him. Phebe was with him, helping, ministering, laboring with him. She was not a slave *for* Paul, but she was laboring *with* him. That makes a big difference. We are not slaves. A servant is not a slave. A servant is someone who is Christ-like. The Bible says we need to be like Christ, thinking of others always.

Historically, women have had a significant role in the Lord's work. We have had a lot of great women in our church. I will name just a few who have gone on to be with the Lord.

Pastor speaks often of Goldie Brown. She was such a blessing and encouragement. She was sick and feeble, but she had the greatest smile and would encourage my husband so much. She was a real servant. She did what she could.

In *Mark 14:6-9*, Jesus said of Mary, *"...She hath wrought a good work on Me...**She hath done what she could**...this also that she hath done shall be spoken of for a memorial of her."*

Sometimes we think we have to be some great person. We get someone in our minds that we want to be just like. We have this picture of who we wish we could be. But most of the time, that is not what the Lord wants us to be. It is okay to incorporate some things from other people, but we each really need to pray and do what we can do. We all can do something in the Lord's work.

Myra Uhlar, one of our dear ladies who is with the Lord now, was a blessing. She was also an encourager. She used to do little things all the time. She would make goodies and bake bread for us. She did what she could. It may not have been anything big or fabulous, but she did her part in the Lord's work. She was also a faithful witness to everyone with whom she came in contact.

Simone Mandeville, another of our dear ladies who went Home to be with the Lord after battling cancer for several years, was a powerful witness for Christ to all who came into her life because of her illness. We have heard the testimonies of the doctors and nurses who knew her.

My husband's mother, Ruby Gaylardo, told everyone about the Lord after she got saved. She witnessed to all of her neighbors, every doctor she went to, and all the nurses. She just did what she could; she did her part. Her doctors and nurses even came to her funeral. That is amazing considering how busy they always are. That was a real testimony for Ruby that the Lord really worked in her life.

Women have a great role in the church. We have a lot of influence. Think of the influence we have with our families. They are the hardest people in the world to have influence with because they know us inside out

and upside-down. I was the first one saved in my family. We were all Catholic. The Lord really used me with my family members, and I am so thankful for that. But I really prayed that they would all be saved, and God gave me influence with them. They have all trusted Christ as their Saviour.

All of us have influence, everywhere we go and with everyone we know. Our coworkers, our families, people are watching us. We have great influence, and we have to remember that.

These women found that the joy of the Lord was serving Jesus in the local church. That is the most important thing and sums it up. We must find the joy of the Lord and serve Him in the local church. We will be blessed for it.

Guidelines for Women in the Church

Everyone has guidelines in their life. Without guidelines we would have anarchy. Everyone has guidelines everywhere they go and in everything they do.

The sports world certainly has guidelines. No one can get out there and do whatever they want to do. The referees would be blowing whistles and calling fouls.

The business world is the same way. None of us can start a new job and say, "Hey! I am going to do this my way." I do not think so. They train us and tell us the way that we are to do the job. This is the way they do it and if we do not like it, there is the door.

Churches have guidelines too. Christians should have guidelines. Everyone has guidelines. There are guidelines in the Bible for women in the church.

Women should be careful not to dominate men in the work of the Lord.

I Timothy 2:12 says, *"But I suffer not a woman to teach, nor to usurp authority over the man, but to be in silence."* This is a very misunderstood verse.

Usurp means to take or assume power or position, by force or without right. To usurp authority means to dominate or have control over.

This is contrary to the world's thinking. The Lord Jesus, warning the disciples about the world's standards and ways in *Matthew 20: 25, 26*, said, *"But it shall not be so among you."* The Lord is saying that Christian standards are not the world's standards. We are to have our own guidelines.

Women should not dominate the leadership in the local church. Phebe was a very strong woman who was filled with God's power, but she did not dominate the Apostle Paul or the leadership in the local church. She was a servant *of* the church, not a servant *over* the church. That is a very important difference.

We can still be strong women. I like to think that I am a strong woman in certain ways. Yet we have to be so careful that we do not dominate the pastor or the local church leadership. I am sorry to say so, but we have had some women come to our church who really tried to run the church and the pastor. I could not believe those women!

Phebe was a servant of the church, not a servant over the church. We as women have a place. The Bible makes it plain and clear.

Women should be sensitive about becoming too outspoken in the Lord's work.

I Corinthians 14:34 and *35* say, *"Let your women keep silence in the churches: for it is not permitted unto them to speak; but they are commanded to be under obedience, as also saith the law. And if they will learn any thing, let them ask their husbands at home: for it is a shame for women to speak in the church."*

I Timothy 2:11 says, *"Let the woman learn in silence with all subjection."*

This does not mean that women cannot sing or speak in church. In context, this teaches that women cannot conduct the services. The Bible plainly teaches that women are not to be pastors. Now, some churches do not agree with that, but that is what the Bible says and teaches. We will not have a problem with that in this church. No way do I want to be the pastor! What thinking woman would?

There are some women who speak out, and that is a problem in some churches sometimes. We have had our share of women who have spoken out, and we have tried to tell them in love that they need to be a little quieter in the service. We know that when the pastor is preaching, it is not a time to have conversation, but we have had that happen sometimes. Sunday school is different, but in the church service women have their place. Everyone has their place actually.

This does not mean that women cannot teach people or that women cannot be Sunday school teachers, but it means that women cannot be preachers. Women can say "Amen!" in the church service and nod their heads and agree with things, but they should not do it loudly.

Women are to adorn themselves in modest apparel.

I Timothy 2:9 and 10 say, "In like manner also, that women adorn themselves in modest apparel, with shamefacedness and sobriety; not with broided hair, or gold, or pearls, or costly array; But (which becometh women professing godliness) with good works."

These verses teach that there ought to be more to a woman than what she wears, how she fixes her hair, and if she is fat or thin. These verses are talking about the inner beauty of a woman. The Bible is clear about teaching women that they ought to be modest, not just in what they wear but also in how they act and what they do. Be modest.

The Lord wants women to adorn themselves in *"modest apparel."* There is nothing wrong with looking sharp or attractive, but there is something wrong with looking sexy. Sexy is a worldly look. Modest apparel means that the clothing does not send the wrong signals or take away from the work of the Lord.

Women who are servants in the local church should be careful that what they wear and how they look does not take away from the truth that they are teaching. If I were teaching while wearing a leather mini-skirt so tight that I could not breathe, with a blouse unbuttoned down too far, I would need to sit down and stop teaching.

Clothing makes a difference. People do not like to think so, but it really does. We are sending signals with our clothing. I believe that every woman wants to be attractive, and we can be sexy at home for our husbands, but when we go out into the world, we need to look attractive, not sexy.

The Apostle Paul said in *I Corinthians 8:13, "Wherefore, if meat make my brother to offend, I will eat no flesh while the world standeth, lest I make my brother to offend."* We need to magnify the Lord in everything that we do. Paul decided that if eating meat offended the brethren, he would not eat it. There is nothing wrong with eating meat but it offended some people. We need to make sure that our clothing does not offend people, especially if we are Christians and we are trying to tell others about Christ.

If we are trying to witness and make a difference in the lives of people, we are going to be judged. That is just the way it is. We need to make sure our clothing does not give the wrong signals to the wrong people. A Christian lady who walks around trying to be sexy is trying to be sexy for other men, and that is not the way Christ wants us to be. We can be attractive, but we need to be careful about it. Wear modest apparel.

The Lord does not give guidelines to women to make their lives difficult. He gives guidelines to help Christian ladies magnify Christ and His work.

The Work of a Woman

Women are to teach other women.

There are three things that women must teach other women. These three things are the hardest things to do in the Christian life. The longer we live the more we realize how difficult it is to win these three victories. We must:

Keep our lives right. *John 8:29* says, *"...for I do always those things that please Him."* The highest goal of a Christian is to please the Lord.

If there is a question about something, we should ask ourselves, "Will this please the Lord?" That will help us out so much in everything we do. If we have a doubt about it, we should not do it. It is as simple as that. Just wait on the Lord and pray and He will show us. We will be glad we did later. If we do not wait on the Lord and we try to do things in our own strength, we are headed down a tough road. Be right with God, and be right with people. We must keep our lives right.

Keep our hearts stirred up. *Proverbs 4:23* is a great verse. We need to mark it in our Bibles. *"Keep thy heart with all diligence; for out of it are the issues of life."* I think of the heart as being our feelings. From our hearts are the issues of life, how our lives are going to turn out.

Feelings are so fickle. We can get up in the morning feeling one way, but half an hour later we can feel another way. It is scary to think that our feelings can lead us and affect the outcome and decisions of our lives. We have to keep our hearts with all diligence for out of the heart are the issues of life.

We should keep our hearts in the work of the Lord. That is so important. "Keep" is an action word. It is not something that is just going to happen. For example, a diet does not just happen. A diet takes hard work and dedication. We have to keep our hearts in the work of the Lord.

We must guard our hearts. What takes a woman's heart? There are three things that can take a woman's heart: failures, forsakers, and fighters.

Failure can take a woman's heart. I can say with confidence that every lady has had failures in her life. We all have had failures. Some of

us have had great failures. Some of us have had little failures. When we fail we think, "This is it. I have really done it now. I have really messed my life up. This is the stupidest thing I have ever done."

I beat myself up when I fail. I was always the kind of child who did not have to be spanked when I did something wrong (even though my mom did) because I was so hard on myself. I would be devastated that I hurt my mother by disobeying. She said I was her angel child. My sisters debate that! I guess I was such an easy child because I had a strong conscience.

Failure takes our courage. It can totally defeat us. When we feel totally defeated, we step back, and then we start withdrawing. We put that wall up. We think, "If one person says one thing to me right now I do not know what I am going to do. I am just going to lose it." We feel that we cannot handle another thing. Soon we are stepping back further and further and further.

What do we need to do when we fail? We have to deal with these failures. The Bible says to keep our hearts with all diligence. I think this is part of what the Bible is talking about. If we do not take care of failure, we will be finished. We will be in a corner, totally defeated. We can get over failures by doing these things.

Take responsibility. The first thing we need to do is take responsibility for our failure. It may not be all our fault but we should ask ourselves, "How can I fix this personally?" If it is sin we first need to confess it and forsake it.

Give it to the Lord. We have to give it to the Lord if we are going to move forward. Tell the Lord, "Lord, I have fixed this as much as I can. I have done all I can do. I am giving this failure to You." We need to pray for our courage back, too.

Step back into life. We withdraw when we have great failures, so we need to step back into life. I have been devastated many times in my life, but the joy of the Lord is my strength. *Nehemiah 8:10* says, *"...The joy of the LORD is your strength."* We must ask the Lord to strengthen and help us, and then get up, step back into the work, and get busy for the Lord.

If we do not get over failure, it piles up on us. Women are like that. We get things piled up so high that we do not even know what is wrong with us. Women are so complicated. So with failure, we need to take responsibility, give it to the Lord, and move on for Him. He will help us with it.

Forsakers can take a woman's heart. We all have been forsaken by someone. Forsakers are people that take our hearts. These are people that we try to help and love and do all we can for. We treat their children like we would our own. Actually, we want more for their children than they want for them. We get so involved. Yet forsakers turn around and leave us. It breaks our hearts when someone we consider a friend just turns around and walks away. It is a terrible thing.

We have had a lot of people come through this church. No matter who it is, every person that leaves breaks my heart. We work so hard to help people, and we establish relationships and friendships, and we just cannot get around that. They take our hearts sometimes. We all know what I am talking about. We have all had our hearts taken from us.

We have to take care of forsakers breaking our hearts too, because if we do not, we become bitter. Bitterness is like a cancer. I have pictures in my mind of people who are so bitter that it shows all over their faces. We can hear it in their voices. We can spot it a mile off. Bitterness is something that we cannot hide.

Circumstances do not make us bitter. It is how we react to them that makes us bitter. If somebody does us wrong, first we are hurt, then we get mad, and then we get really angry. We pray, "Lord, I am doing everything I am supposed to do. I did not do anything wrong in this situation. Why did this person do this to me? I am not going to do this anymore for people."

Get over it. We have to get over things. We have to roll with the punches in life. We have to learn how to react to circumstances. We can cry, "Lord, I do not know why this happened. I do not know why people are so mean. But I know there is a reason." We do not have all the answers. We need to pray, "Lord, my heart is broken, and I want You to help me get over this." We have all been through a lot. Everybody has been through heartaches. The Lord will help us get over it.

Learn from it. Second, I always pray that the Lord will teach me something from each experience. That kind of softens the blow, I think. We learn the most through hard times and experiences. That is what the Bible teaches. In the valleys is where the Lord really speaks to our hearts. We really lean on the Lord, and that is where we learn some valuable lessons. So we need to pray that the Lord will help us learn from difficulties.

Become a better person through it. Third, I always pray that I can become a better person because of each experience. The Lord will answer those prayers. He will make us better people because of the hardships.

So when we have forsakers in our lives that take our hearts, we can pray that God will help us to get over it, learn from it, and become better people through it.

Fighters can take a woman's heart. We must all deal with people who fight against us. Fighters can kill our spirit.

A fighter could be a lost husband that a lady has to deal with every day of her life or every time she comes to church. I know a lot of ladies in this church who have to deal with that. Their husbands fight them, and it is a terrible thing. I have known some ladies who get to church in tears because of the horrible struggle they have to go through to get here.

The fighters could be our children. Some children rule the roost. It is not the Bible way, but it is that way in some homes. We cannot let our children wear us down. We have to stick to our guns and stand our ground because if we do not they are going to defeat us. They do not have the wisdom that we do. God has given children parents for a reason, so we can teach our children.

Michelle and I were at the craft fair the other night. I had bought something earlier at one of the booths, and we were going back to pick it up an hour later. A woman was still there with her child who was screaming in a tantrum. We could hear it two booths away.

There was something for children on top of a piece of furniture, and this child was picking out which one he wanted. His mother was arguing with him saying, "I told you that you can't have that." "But I want it!" he was screaming. She said, "Put it back." Then he screamed louder and louder. He was conquering her.

The poor vendor was a nervous wreck. She must have been there for an hour going through this tantrum.

The mother said again, "Put it back. You're not getting it." We really heard him scream then! So she said, "Okay, pick it out." After that he was even worse.

By the time Michelle and I got out of there, he had made a fool out of her. We could tell that this child actually runs the house. She should have

taken him out and spanked him. Finally she said, "Okay, let's go. We're leaving." She kept screaming and arguing with this child all the way out the door. It was just crazy.

We cannot let our children conquer us. That mother was definitely conquered by that child. She could and should have done something about it. We cannot let our children conquer us. It is going to be hard. Sometimes it is a real fight, but we cannot let them do it. We have to stand our ground.

Others who may fight against us are family members. My family was all Catholic, so when we got saved, they thought we were into some kind of a cult or something. It was really tough.

I used to visit my mom every year. I told her, "Sunday and Wednesday, we are going to church. Are you coming, Mom?" She would say, "No, no, we'll go to Catholic church." I said, "I'm not going to Catholic church, Mom." We just kept praying, and the Lord answered our prayers. All of our family members were eventually saved. What a blessing! Then I would visit and say, "Okay, Mom, we're going to church." She would say, "Okay." What a big change.

We cannot let our family members wear us down. I know lost family members can wear us down. I know a lot of us pray for our lost family members. They can actually be mean to us, but we cannot take it personally. I do not think they are really being mean. They are fearful and concerned. They do not understand what we are involved in. They do not understand the things of the Lord. We know our families.

Keep praying that the Lord will work through circumstances in their lives. They will start listening. Even before my mom accepted the Lord she started listening. If we stand our ground our families will see that what we have is real. That is important.

We used to come down and my mom would say, "You know, I really admire you." I could see the Lord really working in her heart. She knew that even when she would visit us, she would sit in our house alone on Sunday morning because we were gone to church. "Okay, Mom, we're going to church this morning. See you later." She could not believe it.

We must stand our ground. I believe with all my heart that if we did not stand our ground, and we were not faithful to the Lord, my family would not be saved today. If they had conquered me, they would not be saved, because it would not have been real. Our families see a difference in our lives.

My husband and I got saved, because of my husband's brother. At first I thought Clarence's being a pastor was a job he had. I did not understand. I thought, "He has a great job. Look at his house. Look at his car." Then I started watching him and seeing the sacrifices he made and the things that he did and the time he put into it. I thought, "There is something more to this," and I became curious.

This is what our family members go through. They start watching us. Our families respect and love us even though they do not understand. They begin to listen more. That is the Lord working in their hearts. So we must not let family members conquer us.

The devil fights against us. Again, we have to stand our ground. That devil will give us the hardest time. He knows right when to hit us, but we have to remember that we are in the palm of God's hand. The only thing the devil can do to us is what the Lord allows, and there is comfort in that. We just cannot let the devil conquer us.

We have three things that we need to guard our hearts against: the failures in our lives, the forsakers in our lives, and people that fight against

us. We need to guard our hearts, because otherwise we lose our courage, we lose our hearts, and we lose our spirit. That is why this verse is so important. *"Keep thy heart with all diligence; for out of it are the issues of life" (Proverbs 4:23).*

Stay on track. The third thing that women are to teach other women is to stay on track. *"Brethren, I count not myself to have apprehended: but this one thing I do…" (Philippians 3:13).*

Busyness is not always best. That is kind of funny to me, because we are all so busy. We need to narrow our interests. People will love what we love and do what we do. We must live the one-track life. It is so important to get our priorities straight. We are so busy doing so many things. We need to narrow our interests. That will keep us on track.

Women are to teach children and young people.

"And these words, which I command thee this day, shall be in thine heart: And thou shalt teach them diligently unto thy children, and shalt talk of them when thou sittest in thine house, and when thou walkest by the way, and when thou liest down, and when thou risest up" (Deuteronomy 6:6, 7).

It is only when we teach that we truly grow. This is so true. We who have ever taught a Sunday school class know that is when we really grew. We grow when we teach because we have to study more, and therefore we learn more.

Molding a young person's life is one of the greatest things that women can do in the Lord's work. All my Christian life I have heard and read of women who have made such an impact on preachers, missionaries, teachers, and Christian leaders from all walks of life. I do not know of a man or woman that has accomplished great things for God with their life who does not acknowledge the influence of some Christian woman in their childhood or when they were babes in Christ. Dr. Lee Roberson, one of my heroes, tells of his Sunday school teacher who won him to Christ and helped mold him as a young boy.

Romans 16:1 says, *"I commend unto you Phebe our sister, which is a **servant of the church**... "* Phebe knew that the purpose of the Christian life is to be a servant of the Lord. May we all be willing to be servants.

There are many ministries in the local church where women can serve the Lord and make a difference in people's lives. The following lists some of the things we are doing in our church.

Ladies' Ministries

✦ TEACHING MINISTRY
Adult ladies' Sunday school classes, young people, children

Follow-up lessons for new Christians

Training and discipleship lessons

Ladies' Bible studies (covering special subjects)

Christian school (teach and aid)

✦ HOSPITALITY MINISTRY
Welcome committee for new members

Greet visitors and show them around

Send letters and cards to those who have visited our church

Note: *Roll out the red carpet.*

✦ SHUT-IN MINISTRY

Visit shut-ins

Recognize special days for our shut-ins

Send notes and cards for holidays, birthdays and anniversaries

✦ MINISTRY TO THE BEREAVED

Help and assist those who have lost a loved one

Take food to families on the day of a funeral

Send notes and cards for encouragement

✦ TRACT MINISTRY

Hand out tracts

Keep material updated and supplied

Prepare packets for visitors

✦ HOSPITAL MINISTRY

Visit with family while their loved one is having surgery

Visit church members in the hospital

Make sunshine visits to non-members

Send flowers and cards

✦ NEW MOTHERS MINISTRY

Have baby showers

Help new mothers get adjusted

Provide meals for new mothers

✦ NEWLYWEDS MINISTRY

Help young women adjust to married life (planning a budget,
 meals, family schedule, keeping their homes)
Church activities

✦ PRAYER MINISTRY

Ladies' prayer meeting
Keep up-to-date prayer list for church
Pray for sick and shut-ins, special needs of our church
Prayer fellowship (call in time to request prayer)

✦ FOLLOW-UP MINISTRY

Welcome new members
Teach and train new converts
Help all new members to find their place of service

✦ MUSIC MINISTRY

Sing in the choir
Play an instrument in the orchestra
Play piano or organ
Sing specials or sing in a special music group

✦ ENCOURAGEMENT MINISTRY

Write notes to young people who are trying to use their
talents for the Lord
Write notes to Christians who need encouragement
Be an encouragement at church (*Hebrews 3:13*)

✦ **Children's Ministry**

> Teach children's Sunday school
>
> Serve in children's worship service
>
> Teach in children's programs (King's Kids or Master's Club)
>
> Work with the children's choir
>
> Serve in the Christian school as a teacher or volunteer
>
> Write notes to children
>
> Volunteer for junior camp for boys and girls
>
> Help with day trips for children
>
> Work in the bus ministry

✦ **Youth Ministry**

> Teach Sunday school
>
> Help in youth activities
>
> Write notes to young people when they sing or play an instrument in service
>
> Serve at youth camp and special youth meetings
>
> Work with the teen choir
>
> Help with teen visitation

✦ **Missionary Ministry**

> Pray for missionaries and their families
>
> Keep up with mission needs
>
> Send cards and letters
>
> Do special things for birthdays and anniversaries
>
> More is covered in Lesson 4

✦ SOUL-WINNING AND VISITATION MINISTRY

Note: *Being a faithful witness is not an option. All Christians are to be witnesses (Acts 1:8).*

Be involved in the scheduled soul winning outreach of the church (ladies' visitation, church-wide soul winning, etc.)

Follow up with parents of children who have made decisions for the Lord

More is covered in Lesson 6

✦ OTHER MINISTRIES

Landscaping church property

Housekeeping and maintenance of church buildings

Outreach to new residents

Tape ministry - record, copy, and distribute sermon tapes

Sending care packages and encouraging notes to college students

SET APART FOR THE LORD'S WORK

Chapter Three

Romans 16:1, 2, "I commend unto you Phebe our sister, which is a servant of the church which is at Cenchrea: That ye receive her in the Lord, as becometh saints, and that ye assist her in whatsoever business she hath need of you: for she hath been a succourer of many, and of myself also."

When the Lord speaks of Phebe *"as becometh saints,"* He is saying that she was heading forward in her Christian life. She was becoming sanctified, set apart for His use. The Lord is revealing a twofold truth about her life. First He speaks of what He has done *for* her, and second He speaks of what He is doing *through* her.

Philippians 1:6 says, *"Being confident of this very thing, that He which hath begun a good work in you will perform it until the day of Jesus Christ."* God begins a good work in us when we get saved. He continues to work *in* us, and then *through* us, as we follow Him and

surrender our lives to Him. But God can never work *through* us until He has first worked *in* us.

The Christian life is a life of yielding and surrender. We surrender to the Lord and yield to His leadership. Many ladies stop somewhere along life's journey and never reach the level of Christian service the Lord has for them and never accomplish what the Lord has planned for their lives.

According to *Romans 8:28* and *29*, we learn that everything that happens to us will make us more like the Lord Jesus if we surrender to it. *"And we know that all things work together for good to them that love God, to them who are the called according to His purpose. For whom He did foreknow, He also did predestinate to be conformed to the image of His Son, that He might be the firstborn among many brethren."*

Phebe not only knew the Lord and was a wonderful servant in the church, but she was also moving forward in her Christian life. Every serious-minded Christian should ask themselves these questions: Am I going forward in my Christian life and walk? Am I the kind of follower that truly is considered *"as becometh saints"*?

What does it mean to be a saint? Sanctification has to do with what the Lord has done in us, and what we are allowing the Lord to do through us. That is the key word, *allowing*. God cannot do anything in us unless we allow Him to. If we are going to be stiff-necked and stubborn, God cannot work through us. We have a responsibility to let God work in us and through us.

As we study this lesson we will see what the Lord has done for us and what steps we should take in order for the Lord to accomplish His will and work through us.

We Must Understand What the Lord Has Done for Us

In *John 13:12*, the Lord Jesus asks this question: *"Know ye what I have done to you?"* If we were to make a list of what God has done for us, where would we begin? What has the Lord done for us? If we do not think about that, we may take for granted all that God has done. We should take time daily to praise the Lord for working in our lives.

Philippians 1:6 says, *"Being confident of this very thing, that He which hath begun a good work in you will perform it until the day of Jesus Christ."*

The Lord has given us new life.

"And you hath He quickened, who were dead in trespasses and sins" (Ephesians 2:1). Quickened means made alive. God gives us new life, which begins at the second birth, when we are saved.

I received new life on September 14, 1976, when the Lord saved me. God gave me a new start, a second chance. He gave me a new home, a new family. Everything was new. *"Therefore if any man be in Christ, he is a new creature: old things are passed away; behold, all things are become new" (II Corinthians 5:17).*

God has given us new life. What a wonderful gift! We can start all over, brand new and fresh. What a blessing!

The Lord has made us children of light.

John 12:36 says, *"While ye have light, believe in the light, that ye may be the children of light…"* *Ephesians 5:8* says, *"For ye were sometimes darkness, but now are ye light in the Lord: walk as children of light."* Before we were saved we lived in darkness, but now we are living in light, so we need to walk as children of light.

Light comes from God's Word. *Psalm 119:105* says, *"Thy Word is a lamp unto my feet, and a light unto my path."* What a great verse. What have we learned from God's Word since we have been saved?

When I got saved, it was as if God opened my mind. Before my husband and I were saved, we listened to the wrong kind of music. My husband had thousands of dollars' worth of records. I remember one album in particular. I would try to sing along with it, but when I could not understand all the words, I would just sing what I thought I heard.

We got saved in Emmanuel Baptist Church. My husband asked, "Pastor Riley, can we keep the *good* music?" Pastor Riley said, "Listen to the albums that you think are good, and you tell me if you can keep them."

The first record we put to the test had a song that said something like, "All this talk about Jesus. Aw, you couldn't fool us." We had never heard those words before. I said, "Play that again. I can't believe he just said that." We heard it again. "All this talk about Jesus. Aw, you couldn't fool us." We had never heard those words clearly before. We were shocked. It was unbelievable.

God had opened our minds and given us light. It was an amazing miracle. Of course, we soon discovered that we could not keep *any* of our old records. We told Pastor Riley, and he got a big kick out of it.

God gives us light. He opens our minds. The Bible is truly a lamp unto our feet and a light unto our path.

God gave me the verse *Proverbs 3:5, 6* years ago when I was going through a lot of health problems and could not understand why. I am the type of person who tries to figure everything out. Sometimes we cannot figure it out. We will wear ourselves out trying to understand everything. We just need to trust the Lord, and He will guide us. That is why *Proverbs 3:5, 6* is my life verse. *"Trust in the LORD with all thine heart; and lean not unto thine own understanding. In all thy ways acknowledge Him, and He shall direct thy paths."*

Light comes from the Holy Spirit. *I John 2:27* says, *"But the anointing which ye have received of Him abideth in you, and ye need not that any man teach you: but as the same anointing teacheth you of all things, and is truth, and is no lie, and even as it hath taught you, ye shall abide in Him."* This verse is talking about the Holy Spirit teaching us and giving us light. We need to be sensitive to the Holy Spirit.

One thing that causes us to be *in*sensitive to the Holy Spirit is the world. The world is always there, pounding on our door. That is how I picture it. We always have this fight with the world. We need to be sensitive to the things of God.

There are other things that can make us *in*sensitive to the Spirit of God. Listening to wrong music. Watching the wrong things on TV. Going to the wrong places. These will make us cold toward the things of God. We cannot be sensitive to the Holy Spirit and do the things that we should not do.

The Holy Spirit will convict our hearts. Let us be sensitive to the Lord. Phebe was yielded to the Bible and in tune with the Holy Spirit. *Romans 8:16* says, *"The Spirit itself beareth witness with our spirit, that we are the children of God."*

I went to the mall by myself one time in the evening during the holidays when I was very busy. My girls always say, "Mom, don't go to the mall by yourself," but I had to buy some makeup, so I *had* to go to the mall. I got out of my car and was walking in the parking lot towards the store, and suddenly I got this sick feeling. I thought, "I shouldn't be doing this." I sensed danger. I believe it was the Holy Spirit speaking to my heart. I just turned around, got back in my car, and left.

The Holy Spirit, if we are sensitive to Him, can warn us of danger. Have you ever been somewhere and all of a sudden you want to get out? You do not feel right about it, as if something bad is going to happen. That is the Holy Spirit. What a great blessing the Lord has given us. If we are in tune with and sensitive to the Holy Spirit, He can speak to our hearts about so many things.

The Holy Spirit convicts us of bad habits too. As Christians, when we do something wrong, we are the first ones who know it. It is obvious. The Holy Spirit convicts us, so we need to stay in tune.

The Lord has made us children of light. He gives us light from God's Word, and light from the Holy Spirit. The Lord also gives us light from other believers.

Light comes from other believers. *Matthew 5:14* says, *"Ye are the light of the world. A city that is set on an hill cannot be hid."* *I John 1:7* says, *"But if we walk in the light, as He is in the light, we* *have fellowship one with another, and the blood of Jesus Christ His Son cleanseth us from all sin."*

The "other believers" are our spiritual leaders and, most important, our friends. In over twenty years as a pastor's wife, the saddest thing I see is what happens to people when they get around the wrong friends. If we do not choose godly friends, they will pull us down and ruin us and our families. It is the biggest tragedy. Remember, we do not live for ourselves. We all have families, friends, neighbors, people whose lives we touch. If we get around the wrong friends, they will pull us all down.

What is a good friend? Let me give some opposites.

Good friends love the Lord and try to live for Him.

Bad friends can take or leave the Lord. They are hot and cold. They say, "Sure, I love the Lord," but they are not serious. Bad friends will try to live for God as long as they can still do what they want to do. They do not like rules and regulations. They will only go so far, and then they draw the line.

Good friends want the very best for our lives. They are unselfish.

Bad friends try to convince us to do what *they* think we should do. They say, "Forget about praying about decisions. Forget about God's will for your life. You ought to do this. This is what *I* think you need to do."

Good friends tell us in love when we get off track. That takes courage.

Bad friends will not say a word to us when we get off track, because they really do not care about us. Maybe they are glad we are getting off track, because maybe we are becoming more like them.

Good friends love us, pray for us, and try to help us get back on track when we make mistakes.

Bad friends criticize us and cannot wait to tell everybody about it when we make mistakes.

Good Christians can be on track for years and be doing great, and all of a sudden, we wonder what is going wrong with them. They start falling back and going by the wayside. They get off track. What happened? They got around bad friends who were no good for them. What a rough road they are going to travel.

In *Matthew 28:19* and *20*, the Lord says, *"Go ye therefore...Teaching **them** to observe all things... "* Who is "them"? "Them" means people who are saved. Believers are to teach other believers to observe all things.

We must choose our friends wisely, because the child of God needs light to accomplish God's will. We need all three sources: God's Word, the Holy Spirit, and other believers. Let us make sure our friends are godly. Make sure they love us and really care about us. They should want the very best for us no matter how it affects them.

Curtis Hutson said, "Having a common enemy is a poor basis for friendship." Many of us have seen this happen. Someone gets out-of-sorts and bitter and tries to pull down everyone else with them. That is not a good friend. If someone has a problem, they should deal with it. They should not try to poison the water for everyone else.

He also said, "If you want to know who your friends are, just make a mistake." The wrong friends will turn on us. Remember, Samson had twenty companions who destroyed him.

There are so many verses in the Bible about friends. It would be good to do a word study on it.

We have God's Word, the Holy Spirit, and other believers to give us light. If we fall short in any of these three areas, it will hold us back. We need all three things to accomplish God's will in our lives.

We must yield to the Word of God, be sensitive to the Spirit of God, and stay in step with other Christians. Let us take a test. Are we yielded to God's Word? Are we in tune with the Holy Spirit? Are we in fellowship with God's people?

Every believer has been given some light. We are responsible for the light God has given us. *John 1:9* says, *"That was the true Light, which lighteth every man that cometh into the world."*

"...For unto whomsoever much is given, of him shall be much required..." (Luke 12:48). To whom much is given, much *is* required.

My husband gives the illustration of the man who said, "I have to leave this church. I don't want to hear any more truth or light, because I don't want to obey what I'm hearing. The more I hear, the worse it is going to

be for me." How sad that someone smart enough to know that truth would turn away from it. We are responsible for the light we are given.

What God shows us in the light, we should not turn away from in the darkness. That is when we need to stay still and pray and let God show us what He wants us to do.

Light obeyed brings more light, and light disobeyed brings darkness. If we keep disobeying the Lord, we will keep getting colder and colder toward the Holy Spirit.

Romans 1:21 says, *"Because that, when they knew God, they glorified Him not as God, neither were thankful; but became vain in their imaginations, and their foolish heart was darkened."* Because they did not glorify God, nor were thankful, they became vain in their own imaginations, and their foolish hearts were darkened.

What we do with the light God has given us will determine what God does with us. People quit obeying light and their hearts become darkened. If we ignore God's light, our hearts are going to be darkened.

How do we feel toward people who have given us light? To whom are we giving light?

We each are a testimony. I am reminded of the saying, "You are the only Bible some people will ever read." We need to be our best twenty-four hours a day.

When God said Phebe was "as becometh a saint," that meant she obeyed the light He gave her. Anyone who obeys light can be trusted.

The Lord has set us apart from the world.

I Corinthians 6:11 says, *"And such were some of you: but ye are washed, but ye are sanctified, but ye are justified in the name of the Lord Jesus, and by the Spirit of our God."* He has set us apart from the world.

The Lord said that we are *in* the world, but we are not *of* the world. *John 15:19* says, *"If ye were of the world, the world would love his own: but because ye are not of the world, but I have chosen you out of the world, therefore the world hateth you."* I do not think any Christian is going to be voted the best man or woman of the year. That is not possible. If we are being what God wants us to be, we will not be the most popular people in the world. But we should be able to be voted best employee of the month. We should be recognized as good Christians.

A real Christian is not going to fit in with the world. Even though we have to live in the world, we are not *of* the world.

The Lord said that the world would hate us. That is strong language. The Lord said in *John 15:18, "If the world hate you, ye know that it hated Me before it hated you."* If the world hated the Lord, it is going to hate Christians. The only Christian the world loves is the one who is conforming to the world.

People think they can stay neutral. We cannot stay neutral. We are either going forward or backward. When we come to decisions in our lives, we must choose truth. Not to obey means to back up. When we receive truth and do not act on it, we are backing up. Staying neutral does not work. We have to take a stand for what we believe in.

The world is going to push us, test us, and try us. *Romans 12:2* says, *"And be not conformed to this world: but be ye transformed by the renewing of your mind, that ye may prove what is that good, and acceptable, and perfect, will of God."* Do not be *conformed* to this world, but rather be *transformed* by reading the Bible and praying.

The Lord has sanctified us through truth.

John 17:17 says, *"Sanctify them through Thy truth: Thy Word is truth."* How we receive the truth of God's Word determines how much the Lord uses us. Someone once said, "What you do with this Book determines what God does with you." If we study and read God's Word and pray, God can work through us. If we are cold-hearted toward the Lord, how can He work through us?

Sometimes God will lay someone on our hearts. When we are in tune with God's Word and the Holy Spirit, God is able to speak to our hearts. But if we are the kind of Christians who are cold-hearted, and we do not read our Bibles and pray, and we are "hit-and-miss," then God is not going to speak to our hearts.

God wants to have fellowship with us. He wants to speak to our hearts, and He does it through truth. We have to let Him speak to us by being sensitive to Him.

We should HEAR truth. *Romans 10:17* says, *"So then faith cometh by hearing, and hearing by the Word of God."* If we do not hear the Word, we cannot obey the Word. We need to hear truth.

Many times people come to us with problems, but if they are not faithful to church, they miss the very service in which God could have answered their prayer! If we do not hear truth, how can we obey truth? If we come to church three times a week and are faithful to the Lord, we hear and learn so much. Think of how much we can learn in Sunday school classes and church services.

There is so much truth to learn. I can read my Bible and learn, but I like Bible classes, and I love to hear preaching. When my husband and I vacation, we set up in advance where we will go to church. We go from meeting to meeting along our route, and I learn so much. I really love to hear preaching because God speaks to my heart through preaching. We need to hear truth, but if we are not in church to hear it, we are not going to grow as Christians.

We need to be careful what we listen to. *Revelation 1:3* says, *"Blessed is he that readeth, and they that hear the words of this prophecy, and keep those things which are written therein: for the time is at hand."* We need to hear truth.

We should HOLD truth. *II Timothy 1:13* says, *"Hold fast the form of sound words, which thou hast heard of me, in faith and love which is in Christ Jesus."* Many people are turning loose of things today, but once something is turned loose, it is hard to pick up again.

God can speak to our hearts but if we do not write it down, it is gone from our memories. I can listen to a message in which God speaks to my heart, but if I do not take notes, it is gone! I have learned that when God speaks to my heart, I must write it down. Otherwise, by the time I get to my car, I have forgotten it. I always think I will remember, but later I wonder what that point or Bible verse was that God used. I think that is the devil, the prince and power of the air, taking the seed. Remember the parable of the sower in *Mark 4:14, 15: "The sower soweth the Word. And these are they by the way side, where the Word is sown; but when they have heard, Satan cometh immediately, and taketh away the Word that was sown in their hearts."*

We have to hold onto truth. If we let it go, it is hard to pick back up.

We should HIDE truth. *Psalm 119:11* says, *"Thy Word have I hid in mine heart, that I might not sin against Thee."* The devil steals truth so we need to hide truth in our hearts. If we knew that while we were in church one night, a thief was going to break into our homes and steal some of our valuables, would we not hide them before we left the house? If we do not hide God's truth in our hearts, the devil will steal it from us.

To hide truth means to memorize Bible verses. We will find ourselves in situations where we need God's Word, but we cannot get to a Bible. We will wish then that we had learned and memorized more verses.

In times of trouble, my first thoughts are of the Lord and Bible verses and the things of God I have hidden in my heart. During tragedy, when we are devastated, we will need to remember verses to encourage ourselves in the Lord. Let us hide God's Word, the truth, in our hearts. If we memorize Scripture and hide it in our hearts, the devil cannot take it.

We should HEED the truth. In *Matthew 7:24*, the Lord says, *"Therefore whosoever heareth these sayings of Mine, and doeth them, I will liken him unto a wise man, which built his house upon a rock."* I love the song the children sing, "The Wise Man Built His House Upon A Rock." Some people, sad to say, build their houses upon the sand, and their houses crumble because they have no foundation, no firm ground, no root. We should heed the truth.

Truth cannot change our lives if we do not hear it, hold it, hide it in our hearts, and heed it. Phebe was a woman who had received truth with a surrendered life. The Lord sanctifies us through truth.

✦ We must **HEAR** truth.
✦ We must **HOLD** truth.
✦ We must **HIDE** truth.
✦ We must **HEED** truth.

The Lord begins a work in our lives the day we are saved and continues to work in our lives until death or the Rapture. *"Being confident of this very thing, that He which hath begun a good work in you will perform it until the day of Jesus Christ" (Philippians 1:6).* We must hold onto these things for God to use us.

I thank the Lord for the truth He gives us, and that it is so practical that we can live victorious Christian lives if we are sensitive to the Holy Spirit and have open minds and tender hearts. I pray that we will want to live for the Lord and heed His Word that He gives us every day as we go out into the world trying to do God's will for our lives.

We Must Set Ourselves Apart for the Lord's Use

Joshua 3:5 says, *"And Joshua said unto the people, Sanctify yourselves: for to morrow the LORD will do wonders among you."*

In *Romans 12:1, 2* God says to *"...present your bodies a living sacrifice..."*

We have seen what the Lord does in getting us to the place where we can be used. He has given us new life, and has made us children of light. He has set us apart from the world, and has sanctified us through the truth.

Now we will discuss our part in being set apart. We must be willing to sanctify ourselves. There are four steps to setting ourselves apart for the Lord's use. Ladies who do not take all four steps greatly limit what the Lord can do in and through them.

Step one: We must surrender our lives by giving ourselves to the Lord.

Romans 12:1 and *2* say, *"I beseech you therefore, brethren, by the mercies of God, that ye present your bodies a living sacrifice, holy, acceptable unto God, which is your reasonable service. And be not conformed to this world: but be ye transformed by the renewing of your mind, that ye may prove what is that good, and acceptable, and perfect, will of God."*

In *Mark 8:35* the Lord Jesus says, *"For whosoever will save his life shall lose it; but whosoever shall lose his life for My sake and the gospel's, the same shall save it."*

Pastor often reminds us that the level of our Christian service is determined by the depth of our personal surrender.

First, we must present our bodies as a living sacrifice. When we do this, no longer are we being conformed to this world, but we begin to be transformed by God and His Word.

Everyone is going in one direction or the other. No one stays neutral. Daily we are either conforming to the world, or we are being transformed by God.

This means we are willing to remove those things that are worldly in our lives, the things that will limit our witness for Christ, the things in our lives that the unsaved person would find offensive so as to not listen to our witness. Anyone who has tried to witness can tell of those who have been turned off to the gospel because of the offensive lifestyle of some Christians.

The first step in setting ourselves apart for the Lord is to give our lives to the Lord. The secret to the victorious Christian life is surrender. Phebe was a woman who had surrendered her life to the Lord. We limit how much the Lord can do in our lives when we fail to surrender.

Step two: We must remove the things that limit us.

Hebrews 12:1 and 2 say, "Wherefore seeing we also are compassed about with so great a cloud of witnesses, let us lay aside every weight, and the sin which doth so easily beset us, and let us run with patience the race that is set before us, Looking unto Jesus the author and finisher of our faith; who for the joy that was set before Him endured the cross, despising the shame, and is set down at the right hand of the throne of God."

We should lay aside sin. *John 8:34 says, "Jesus answered them, Verily, verily, I say unto you, Whosoever committeth sin is the servant of sin."*

Matthew 1:21 says, "And she shall bring forth a son, and thou shalt call His name JESUS: for He shall save His people from their sins."

As Christians, we should be willing to lay aside anything that hurts our testimony for Christ. Winning personal victories over bad habits not only encourages our hearts, but also speaks volumes to our friends and loved ones about Christ's power to deliver. Ladies who win personal victories are able to help other women with the battles they fight.

We should lay aside weights. *Philippians 3:13 and 14 say, "Brethren, I count not myself to have apprehended: but **this one thing I do**, forgetting those things which are behind, and reaching forth unto those things which are before, I press toward the mark for the prize of the high calling of God in Christ Jesus."*

The second step is to remove not only the sin in our lives, but the weight. We should be willing, if necessary, to lay aside some good things that keep us from doing the best things with our lives.

There are many things that would not necessarily be sinful to the child of God, but because of what we desire to do for the Lord, they become weights. There are a lot of good things that go on in our churches and communities that take us from the main thing. We must learn how to say no to the things that tie us up and keep us from doing God's will. I know ladies who are involved in sporting events, community projects, politics, et cetera, and have no time to do what is dearest to the heart of our Saviour, and that is to make Christ known.

Many Christians will lay aside sin. They will work to win the victory over some personal habit that is not honoring to the Lord and harms their health, but when we talk about laying aside some good things that have become weights in the Lord's work, they have a real problem. It is heartbreaking to see those who go through life picking up weights and who then slowly disappear from the battlefield for God.

Most of the good things we are doing outside the church will go on without us, but the lost will never have a chance to hear without us. Many will never be in Heaven because Christians have become too involved in things that take their time and energy away from sharing the gospel.

We should come to the place in our walk with the Lord where we say, "I am going to lay aside this weight for the gospel." The result will be souls saved and joy in Heaven.

We limit how effective our witness will be to the lost when we do not lay aside the sin and weight. Phebe was a woman who had removed the things that held her back.

Step three: We must abstain from things that limit our influence with other Christians.

I Corinthians 8:9 says, *"But take heed lest by any means this liberty of yours become a stumblingblock to them that are weak."*

I Corinthians 8:13 says, *"Wherefore, if meat make my brother to offend, I will eat no flesh while the world standeth, lest I make my brother to offend."*

The third step is to make sure that we do not limit our influence with God's people. We must be careful that our liberty does not become a stumbling block to the weaker sister.

We must always be on guard for the things that limit our influence with other Christians. We lead people and motivate others with our influence. There are things such as poor personal appearance, tardiness, rudeness, or a lack of joy that can weaken our influence.

Ladies who understand the work of the Lord will also care what other Christians think of them. Our lives should be a testimony and challenge to others to be their best for Christ and to follow our example. Paul said in *I Corinthians 4:16, "Wherefore I beseech you, be ye followers of me."*

How much do we want God to use us to stir the hearts of His people? The question is answered with how much we are willing to give up for the gospel.

If we do not take the third step and remove things that are offensive to God's people, we limit our influence and ability to challenge other believers to be involved in the work of the Lord. Phebe was a woman who had influence with God's people because she was willing to remove the things that limited her with other Christians.

Step four: We must accept the responsibility for our lives and the Lord's work.

Romans 9:1-3 say, *"I say the truth in Christ, I lie not, my conscience also bearing me witness in the Holy Ghost, That I have great heaviness and continual sorrow in my heart. For I could wish that myself were accursed from Christ for my brethren, my kinsmen according to the flesh."* Paul said that he was willing to go to a devil's hell for his kinsmen. We reach the final step of separation *"unto the gospel"* when we are willing to accept the responsibility for those we have an opportunity to tell about Christ.

The fourth and final step is a willingness to accept the responsibility for the salvation of the lost. The greatness of our lives will be measured by the opportunity given to us and our willingness to accept responsibility.

Dr. Curtis Hutson used to say, "This generation of Christians is responsible for this generation of lost people." In other words, we are responsible to make sure the gospel is preached to every creature. *"...Go ye into all the world, and preach the gospel to every creature"* *(Mark 16:15).*

We will all give an account of our lives to Christ. *"For we must all appear before the judgment seat of Christ; that every one may receive the things done in his body, according to that he hath done, whether it be good or bad"* *(II Corinthians 5:10).*

God wants us to live a life separated unto the gospel. That means we should give ourselves to the Lord. Then we should lay aside what keeps us from doing the main thing. We should also be careful not to limit ourselves in the area of personal influence. Finally, we should accept the responsibility of telling our generation the message of Christ.

We limit the work of the Lord when we do not accept the responsibility of getting it done. Phebe was a woman who accepted great responsibility and therefore was given great opportunity.

Phebe was *"as becometh saints"* because she understood what the Lord had done in her life and she was willing to let the Lord continue to work in her life.

SENT BY THE LORD

Chapter Four

Romans 16:1, 2, "I commend unto you Phebe our sister, which is a servant of the church which is at Cenchrea: That ye receive her in the Lord, as becometh saints, and that ye assist her in whatsoever business she hath need of you: for she hath been a succourer of many, and of myself also."

The Lord told this church at Rome, which was a missionary church planted by Paul, to *"receive"* and *"assist"* Phebe. The Lord sent her there on His business. God put something in her heart that He wanted accomplished. *Exodus 31:6* says, *"...and in the hearts of all that are wise hearted I have put wisdom..."*

Phebe had something in her heart that God had given her to do for Him. She not only was a sister in the Lord, a sweet and loving servant in her home church at Cenchrea, and was moving forward in her Christian life, but she also had a heart for missions. That is what we all need: a heart for missions.

The work of the Lord is not something we hold in our hands. It is something we have in our hearts. Phebe had something in her heart that the church could benefit from. She was able to get hold of something that many Christians miss: She loved the work of the Lord.

Nothing is closer to the heart of God than taking the gospel to the whole world. *Mark 16:15* says, *"And He said unto them, Go ye into all the world, and preach the gospel to every creature."*

The Bible says that God so loved the world that He gave. *John 3:16* says, *"For God so loved the world, that He gave His only begotten Son, that whosoever believeth in Him should not perish, but have everlasting life."* If we love the Lord and His work we will give. We must give ourselves to the great work of missions. The Lord will always use people who love Him.

There is still much that can be accomplished in missions, and the Lord is looking for Christians with a heart for His work to accomplish it. Phebe had a heart for the Lord and His work, and that is why He sent her. How can we develop more of a heart for missions? As we study this lesson may we give ourselves to the Lord.

We Must See the Big Picture
(God's Plan)

We have to see the "Big Picture," which is God's Plan. *II Peter 3:9* says, *"The Lord is not slack concerning His promise, as some men* *count slackness; but is longsuffering to us-ward, **not willing that any should perish, but that all should come to repentance.*** God is not willing that any should perish but that all might come to repentance and faith in the Lord Jesus.

God's Plan is that everyone be saved. The Bible says that He is not willing that any should perish. The Lord Jesus came into this world *"...to seek and to save that which was lost..." (Luke 19:10).*

We must see the Big Picture, God's Plan. The Apostle Paul prayed, *"That the God of our Lord Jesus Christ, the Father of glory, may give unto you the spirit of wisdom and revelation in the knowledge of Him: **The eyes of your understanding being enlightened**; that ye may know what is the hope of His calling, and what the riches of the glory of His inheritance in the saints, And what is the exceeding greatness of His power to us-ward who believe, according to the working of His mighty power" (Ephesians 1:17-19).*

"The eyes of your understanding being enlightened." We should pray that prayer ourselves, that the eyes of our understanding would be enlightened.

Proverbs 29:18 says, *"Where there is no vision, the people perish: but he that keepeth the law, happy is he."* We must have vision. We know that where there is no vision, people perish.

When we started this church in our apartment, I am sure some of the people who came to visit us thought this was a small-time, mom-and-pop operation. However, we had a vision. We could see a bigger picture. Some people did not stay with us as we moved from building to building and place to place. Some of them just did not see the big picture. They did not understand. Many did stay with us. They saw the big picture

then, and an even bigger picture ahead. We have a bigger picture of our church, a bigger vision. We want to do more for God, so we have to keep our eyes on the big picture.

Acts 1:8 says, *"But ye shall receive power, after that the Holy Ghost is come upon you: and ye shall be witnesses unto Me **both** in Jerusalem, and in all Judea, and in Samaria, and unto the uttermost part of the earth."* The key word is *both*. That means at the same time.

There are four areas in this verse that help us see the big picture. These four areas include both home and foreign missions. How do we see the work of the Lord?

"Jerusalem" — *our home.*

*"Ye shall be witnesses unto Me both in **Jerusalem**..."* The first area is Jerusalem, our home and our home church. We are to provide a faithful witness where we live. Ladies should be involved in God's work at home and in the local church.

There are many things to get involved in where help is needed. We each should pray and ask the Lord to show us what He wants us to get involved in. That is what it is all about, doing the work of the Lord. We need to think about being servants in our own home church.

"Judea" — *surrounding area.*

*"Ye shall be witnesses unto Me...in all **Judea**..."* The second area in this verse is Judea, the surrounding area. We are to provide a faithful witness to those who live nearby. That means going out visiting, knocking on doors, and inviting other people to come to church. We each should pray about a time when we can visit.

If we do not invite people, they are not going to come. Some people just walk into church off the street, but that is rare. That is just not the way people are. They usually have to be invited.

In London, we had a tour guide who stayed with us the whole time, so we took it for granted that she would come to church with us on Sunday as well. Pastor Sexton said, "Now, Sally, you are coming to church with us, aren't you?" She said, "Oh! Pastor Sexton, I am so excited. I was waiting for you to invite me." We thought, "Wow! She was hoping we would invite her." Then we asked the bus driver, and he said, "Yes, I would love to come. I was just waiting for you to invite me." That really stuck with my husband and me.

We assume that people know they are invited and welcome, but they do not know. People like invitations, and they are waiting for us to invite them. We need to go out there and invite people to come to our church, because they need to know the Lord.

"Samaria" — *our country.*

*"Ye shall be witnesses unto Me…in **Samaria**…"* The third area where we must see more of the big picture is Samaria, our country, our homeland. We are to provide a faithful witness to our nation.

My husband and I came to Cape Coral as missionaries and planted the Gulf Coast Baptist Church. Cape Coral is a mission field. When we knock on doors here and talk to people about being saved and going to Heaven they do not know what we are talking about. "Saved? What does that mean?" This is a true mission field.

There are many mission fields in America. We need to be missionaries. We need to go and witness to people and give out tracts and be the missionaries here in our homeland.

There are pockets of people all across our nation who need to be reached with the gospel. Many of these are in different language groups. They can be reached through home missions by the local church.

"The uttermost part of the earth" — *foreign lands.*

"Ye shall be witnesses unto Me...unto **the uttermost part of the earth**. " The fourth area is the uttermost part of the earth, that is, foreign lands. We are to provide a faithful witness to all people.

All people are precious to God. Their souls are eternal. *"For God so loved the world..." (John 3:16).* *"And He said unto them, Go ye into all the world, and preach the gospel to every creature" (Mark 16:15).*

The Bible says we are to be witnesses to all four areas: our home, surrounding areas, our country, and foreign lands. *"Ye shall be witnesses unto Me* **both** *in Jerusalem, and in all Judea, and in Samaria, and unto the uttermost part of the earth."* In *Acts 1:8* we are told to be witnesses *both.* Both means all at the same time. We are to be involved in all four areas at the same time.

People have a tendency to focus on their problems and not their potential. To see the big picture, we cannot focus on our problems. We need to focus on the big picture, God's plan. It is only after we get our eyes off ourselves that we can begin to understand the heart of God. If we focus on our problems, not our potential, we will never see the big picture of God's work.

Do you think that Phebe had problems? The Bible does not say so, but Phebe had problems. Of course she did! If she was living and breathing she had problems. *Job 14:1* says, *"Man that is born of a woman is of few days, and full of trouble."* Do you think the church she attended had problems? Of course. However, problems did not keep Phebe from seeing the big picture.

We must keep our eyes off of ourselves and on the Lord to see the big picture. Phebe could see the big picture.

We need to see the big picture: missions in our home, surrounding areas, our country, and foreign lands. We are to be faithful witnesses in all four areas at the same time.

We Must See Our Responsibility in God's Plan

Ephesians 1:18 says, *"The eyes of your understanding being enlightened; **that ye may know what is the hope of His calling**, and what the riches of the glory of His inheritance in the saints."*

"That ye may know what is the hope of His calling." There is a job for everyone in our missionary program. What can we do?

We can pray for missions.

I Samuel 12:23 says, *"Moreover as for me, God forbid that I should sin against the LORD in ceasing to pray for you: but I will teach you the good and the right way."* It is a sin not to pray for people. We should never stop praying for missions.

Prayer unites us. *Romans 15:30* says, *"Now I beseech you, brethren, for the Lord Jesus Christ's sake, and for the love of the Spirit, that ye strive together with me in your prayers to God for*

me." There is such division today. God gives us something to unite us, and that is prayer. *"Strive **together with me** in your prayers."* To strive together means to unite together. When we pray for people, we develop a bond with them. If we prayed more, there would be less division in our churches.

Sometimes we take prayer so lightly, yet prayer is so important. Prayer changes things. We need to learn to pray more. *Luke 11:1* says, *"And it came to pass, that, as He was praying in a certain place, when He ceased, one of His disciples said unto Him, Lord, teach us to pray..."*

We need to pray for our missionaries on the foreign field. Our prayers are so important to them. They are away from home, away from their families. There are so many hardships they face. We need to make sure that we pray for them every day.

When we pray for our missionaries, we *"strive together"* in the work with them. We have a part in it. We may not be able to go on the mission field, but we can pray for missionaries faithfully, and we can get involved. Choose a missionary family and correspond with them personally. Record their birthdays, anniversaries, and other special events on your calendar and send them cards. There are many things we can do.

Have a bond with them in prayer. Write their names down on your prayer list. If you write to them and tell them you are praying for them, they will usually write you back. That is a bond that you will have forever with them.

Prayer frees and empowers the Word of God. *II Thessalonians 3:1* says, *"Finally, brethren, pray for us, that the Word of the Lord may have free course, and be glorified, even as it is with you."* When we pray, the Word of God has free course.

There is power in prayer. When we pray for missionaries, the Word of God does a work in people's lives. That is how people are saved. We need to pray for people, for our loved ones, for the preacher, for Sunday school teachers, for our church. We need to pray that God would do a work in people's lives.

Isaiah 55:11 says, *"So shall My Word be that goeth forth out of My mouth: it shall not return unto Me void, but it shall accomplish that which I please, and it shall prosper in the thing whereto I sent it."* The Word of God will never return void or empty. Isn't that great! That is such a comfort to me. When we give someone a tract, or read verses to children, we can know it is penetrating, because the Bible is alive. God promises His Word will prosper and accomplish what He pleases. We need to pray that the Word of God will heal and deliver people.

Prayer spares the lives of people. Moses prayed for people, and God spared them in *Exodus 32:9-14*. Verse *11* says, *"And Moses besought the LORD..."* Verse *14* continues, *"And the LORD repented of the evil which He thought to do unto His people."* God was going to consume His people, but Moses prayed for them, and God spared their lives.

How many times might our prayers have spared lives? We do not know what people are going through. For years I knew a wayward woman. I prayed for her constantly, and there were many times (she told me later) that she almost died because of her lifestyle. Maybe she lived because I prayed at that moment. Look at what God did for Moses. He will do the same for us. He spares people's lives.

Lot, as pitiful as he was, prayed, and God spared a city. I always think of Lot as the most pitiful of God's people, but God spared a city because of his prayers. In *Genesis 19:21*, the Lord said, *"...I will not overthrow this city, for the which thou hast spoken."*

Our prayers could spare the lives of people. When we pray for missionaries, the lives of the ones they are working with are affected. If we pray for them, more souls will be saved. God will answer our prayers.

God cared enough about Moses' prayers and Lot's prayers, and He cares enough about our prayers. *"Casting all your care upon Him; for He careth for you" (I Peter 5:7).* It is a shame we have to wait until we are so burdened or broken about something before we really take the time to pray and get a hold of God. We need to pray that way all the time, not just when we are in a crisis. If we have that close relationship with the Lord every day, when something really goes bad in our lives, we will already have that open communication with Him. God tells us to *"Pray without ceasing" (I Thessalonians 5:17).*

I have had a few people since I have been a pastor's wife ask me, "Please pray for me; I cannot pray for myself." I have always thought that was so sad. I have asked them, "You cannot pray for yourself? Are you saved? Are you sure you know the Lord?" They reply, "Yes, I just cannot pray for myself or for my children right now."

God really loves us. He cares about us. We need to pray for everything. (I even pray for parking places! Did you ever go downtown and try to find a parking place?) When God answers our prayers, we are always so amazed. We pray for little things, and God answers our prayers; just think what God would do if we prayed for big things.

Prayer is kept by the Lord. *Revelation 5:8* says, *"And when He had taken the book, the four beasts and four and twenty elders fell down before the Lamb, having every one of them harps, and golden vials full of odours, which are the prayers of saints."* God keeps our prayers in a vial.

Psalm 56:8 tells us that God also keeps our tears in a bottle and our works in a book. *"Thou tellest my wanderings: put thou my tears into Thy bottle: are they not in Thy book?"* I love that verse.

God loves us so much that He keeps our tears in a bottle, our works in a book, and our prayers in a vial or a vase. The prayers of saints are kept by God for a certain time. How many prayers do we have waiting for us at the Judgment Seat of Christ?

Our responsibility in God's plan is to pray for missions. Prayer unites us. Prayer frees and empowers the Word of God. Prayer spares the lives of people. Prayers are kept by the Lord. That is precious to know.

We can give of our income toward missions.

We can give of our income toward missions. We *must* give. It is a commandment of the Lord. The work is not going to be done if we do not give. We must give to the work of the Lord.

Read *Philippians 4:10-18*. Here is verse *10*: *"But I rejoiced in the Lord greatly, that now at the last your care of me hath flourished again; wherein ye were also careful, but ye lacked opportunity."* The church at Philippi sent a special offering to the Apostle Paul, and Paul could not have done it without their offering. God used His people to help Paul.

Philippians 4:18 says, *"But I have all, and abound: I am full, having received of Epaphroditus the things which were sent from you, an odour of a sweet smell, a sacrifice acceptable, wellpleasing to God."* The Apostle Paul said that the offering was well accepted, *"wellpleasing to God."*

We need to test the Lord in tithing. He will provide. God promises in *Malachi 3:10, "Bring ye all the tithes into the storehouse, that there*

*may be meat in Mine house, and **prove Me now herewith, saith the LORD of hosts**, if I will not open you the windows of heaven, and pour you out a blessing, that there shall not be room enough to receive it."*

We can never give too much. *Philippians 4:19 says, "But my God shall supply all your need according to His riches in glory by Christ Jesus."* We cannot out-give the Lord.

We were saved at Emmanuel Baptist Church during a time when Pastor Riley was taking a special offering for missions. My husband and I were having a difficult time financially. We just prayed that we could put two hundred dollars in the offering, but we did not have a chance of coming up with it ourselves. There was nothing we could do. Then my husband's boss called him into the office and said, "You worked overtime—I don't know when—and here is a two hundred dollar check." We could hardly believe it! It was so exciting to see God provide! God will do things like that. God works miracles. He always does it in His way so we know it is His doing, not ours. We need to test God in giving. Prove Him.

God will bless us for having a part in getting the gospel to the poor. That is why the Lord blessed the church we attended in college, Highland Park Baptist Church, pastored by Dr. Lee Roberson. They loved poor people. They were always giving to the poor. They supported so many missionaries that they displayed a map of the world with little red pegs in all the places where they had missionaries. They supported hundreds of missionaries. We need to love the poor. God will bless us for it.

God blesses a church where people love the poor. We try to do that in our church. For example, our bus ministry keeps us right there before people. We love the children and want to see their families saved. Then these dear people get in our hearts. It is a lot of work and a real sacrifice, but God truly blesses our bus workers and our church.

This is what it is all about: getting people in our hearts, missions, going out and telling people, being witnesses. There are promises for those who remember and care for the poor, taking the gospel to them. This is what our missionaries are doing. This is what we all need to do.

Promises for those who remember and care for the poor, taking the gospel to them:

God will bless our lives. If we remember the poor, God will bless our lives. *Luke 14:12-14* says, *"Then said He also to him that bade Him, When thou makest a dinner or a supper, call not thy friends, nor thy brethren, neither thy kinsmen, nor thy rich neighbours; lest they also bid thee again, and a recompence be made thee. But when thou makest a feast, call the poor, the maimed, the lame, the blind: And thou shalt be blessed; for they cannot recompense thee: for thou shalt be recompensed at the resurrection of the just."* We need to remember the poor and take the gospel to them.

We will have treasures in Heaven. If we take the gospel to the poor, we will have treasures in Heaven. *Matthew 19:21* says, *"Jesus said unto him, If thou wilt be perfect, go and sell that thou hast, and give to the poor, and thou shalt have treasure in heaven: and come and follow Me."*

The treasures in Heaven are people. If we think of people as treasures, then we will not get caught up in all these things in the world today. We get so out of focus sometimes. We just "spin our wheels." If people are treasures in Heaven, then we need to get out there and make sure more people go to Heaven with us. Lester Roloff used to say, "I have never seen a hearse pulling a U-Haul. You cannot take your money and your 'things' with you." The only thing we can take with us is people. Family, loved ones, friends, neighbors: these are the treasures in Heaven.

We will be happy and have the joy of the Lord. If we remember the poor, we will be happy and have the joy of the Lord. *Proverbs 14:21* says, *"He that despiseth his neighbour sinneth: but he that hath mercy on the poor, happy is he."* Have mercy on the poor. There are a lot of unhappy Christians. The problem is that we get selfish with our time, our talents, and our money. If we put others first, we will be happy and have the joy of the Lord.

God will repay us and replenish our finances. *Proverbs 19:17* says, *"He that hath pity upon the poor lendeth unto the LORD; and that which he hath given will He pay him again."* God wants us to give to the poor. God does not want them to do without. He means not only financially, but more than that. If you see someone on the street who is homeless, money is not their answer. They need more than that. First, they need the gospel. They need to be saved and get their life right. Then they need to follow steps. *"But seek ye **first** the kingdom of God, and His righteousness; and all these things shall be added unto you"* *(Matthew 6:33).*

God will hear us when we call on Him in prayer. *Proverbs 21:13* says, *"Whoso stoppeth his ears at the cry of the poor, he also shall cry himself, but shall not be heard."* God wants His people to hear the cry of the poor. What are they crying? They cry, *"No man cared for my soul" (Psalm 142:4).* What does a poor person need the most? Sometimes we just look at their physical needs, but most importantly they need the Lord. It does not matter if we gave them a million dollars. Nothing is going to start going right in their lives until they accept the Lord into their hearts. How will they do that? We have to get out there and give out tracts. We have to witness and invite people to church. They are not just going to stumble onto this church and fall in at the door. Sometimes that happens but not often. If we remember the poor, God will hear us when we call on Him in prayer. That is what we want. We do not want to stop the ears of the Lord from hearing us.

We shall not lack in our personal lives. *Proverbs 28:27* says, *"He that giveth unto the poor shall not lack: but he that hideth his eyes shall have many a curse."* I do not want a curse on my life, do you? Is anything lacking in your life? We do not give to get, but when we give, we will not lack. We shall not lack in our personal lives if we give to the poor.

The Lord will deliver us in the time of our trouble. *Psalm 41:1-3* says, *"Blessed is he that considereth the poor: the LORD will deliver him in time of trouble. The LORD will preserve him, and keep him alive; and he shall be blessed upon the earth: and Thou wilt not deliver him unto the will of his enemies. The LORD will strengthen him upon the bed of languishing: Thou wilt make all his bed in his sickness."*

Our lives are full of trouble. *Job 14:1* says, *"Man that is born of a woman is of few days, and full of trouble."* Are we born of women? Yes. Then there will be trouble in our lives. There is no doubt about it. Some time in our lives we will need deliverance. We may need deliverance from the devil or from debt or from disease. If we remember the poor, the Lord will deliver us in time of trouble. *"Blessed is he that considereth the poor: the LORD will deliver him in time of trouble."* This is not insurance. This is assurance.

We can give of our possessions.

Philippians 4:18 says, *"But I have all, and abound: I am full, having received of Epaphroditus the things which were sent from you, an odour of a sweet smell, a sacrifice acceptable, wellpleasing to God."* We should stay informed of the things that are needed by our missionary families. They have specific needs and many times we have what they need. Often things can be shipped for less than they can be purchased for on the field.

We can remember our missionary families on their birthdays, anniversaries and special holidays.

Proverbs 15:23 says, *"...A word spoken in due season, how good is it!"* *Proverbs 16:24* says, *"Pleasant words are as an honeycomb, sweet to the soul, and health to the bones."* Did you ever get a note or a card at just the right time? It really is special. We like it when others remember us, so we need to do the same to others. Ladies can encourage missionary families by staying in touch and by keeping our church informed of their needs. Special cards can be sent from our Sunday school classes.

We can plan special mission trips.

Luke 8:1-3 says, *"And it came to pass afterward, that He went throughout every city and village, preaching and shewing the glad tidings of the kingdom of God: and the twelve were with Him,* ***And certain women***, *which had been healed of evil spirits and infirmities, Mary called Magdalene, out of whom went seven devils, And Joanna the wife of Chuza Herod's steward, and Susanna, and many others, which ministered unto Him of their substance."*

"And certain women..." The Lord allowed these women to go on a mission trip to Galilee. Paul allowed Phebe to go on a mission trip to Rome. Many ladies could go and be a blessing to missionaries and their people. Plan some missionary trips.

We can plan missionary trips like we plan vacations. We can go where we want. If we go on a vacation, we plan it. Some of the ladies in our church go on a mission trip nearly every year, with the purpose of seeing people saved. They count that as their vacation. Our church youth group has gone to several mission fields and helped our missionaries by witnessing and being a blessing. One lady in our church went to Mexico and said that it changed her life because she realized she had so much, while the people in Mexico had so little.

What an encouragement you are to missionaries when you visit their home on the field. You are never the same afterward.

Our pastor went to the Philippines on one mission trip and came back so stirred that he could not speak of it for days. He finally told me about it with tears in his eyes. He said his life would never be the same.

He went to preach in meetings, and the people were already there, waiting for him. They had traveled for days just to hear him preach. Their facilities were very limited so many people had to stand outside to hear him. The weather was very hot, and they would give him cold washcloths and fan him with big fans while he was preaching. They would beg, "Preach more! Preach more!" They wanted to be there all night long. Pastor would preach one sermon, and they would beg him for more, so he would preach another sermon. It was unbelievable. The preaching of God's Word meant everything to them.

They would ask for Bibles and gospel tracts. They thought Bibles and tracts were the most precious things because they loved the Word of God.

Pastor showed me photographs of the homes in the Philippines. Many of the floors are dirt. There is no electricity in some of the villages. But these people love the Lord and have a heart for the work of the Lord.

If our people could only see the fields where our missionaries are serving, our churches would be transformed.

We took a trip to England and Scotland to preach and win people to the Lord. We visited all these little towns and there was not one church.

We went from town to town. They are very spread out over a lot of land. Each town was so quaint, but there were no churches. None. Those people are open to the gospel.

Think of how many churches are in America, yet Christians fight and get mad and go to another church. People change churches like women change purses. It is sad but true. The reasons people leave churches would be hilarious if they were not so sad. People leave churches over the stupidest, little, insignificant things or miscommunications. Think of people in other countries who have no church to attend.

We cannot comprehend it unless we go. It is such a blessing to go to the foreign field. Set up some mission trips in the future. It would be exciting to see what is going on in different places of the world. Think about our missionaries and what we can do to be more of a blessing to them.

We Should Develop a Heart for Others

Philippians 1:21 says, *"For to me to live is Christ, and to die is gain."* Phebe had the privilege of serving and working with one of God's choice servants. She also had the privilege of being part of a great church that was making a difference in the lives of people. That is our goal. One of our church's mottoes is, "Making a difference in the lives of people."

What made Phebe so valuable to the Lord was that she had a heart for the Lord's work. It will not be right if our hearts are not in it.

Philippians 2:20 says, *"For I have no man likeminded, who will naturally care for your state."* Did you ever do something that you did not want to do? Your heart was not in it so you did it grudgingly. You just wanted to get it done and over with. We need to put our hearts into the Lord's work. We have to work at it and pray about it. We need to have a heart for the work.

We can live in one of two places. We have a choice to live in either *Philippians 1:21, "For me to live is Christ, and to die is gain"*; or to live in *Philippians 2:21, "For all seek their own, not the things which are Jesus Christ's."* What makes a woman valuable is her choosing to live in *Philippians 1:21.*

Too many Christians live in *Philippians 2:21, "For all seek their own..."* They have their own lives, their own things they are doing, and they do not think of the Lord. They do not think, *"For me to live is Christ, and to die is gain."*

How many of us really believe that to die is gain? When we put it all in perspective, what is the most important thing? *"For me to live is Christ, and to die is gain."* We are either living for Christ or we are living for ourselves. We need to ask the Lord to help us put our hearts in His work.

People put their hearts in different things. I think a true fisherman is one you can call at two o'clock in the morning, and he will get up and get his fishing pole and go. True golfers are the same way. They will play golf at any time, any place. They are ready to go. People are like that with other sports. They live, eat, and breathe sports. That is all they think about. But we need to put our hearts into the Lord's work.

People with a heart for missions make a church a great church. A church is not a building. A church is people. A church is not going to be

any better than the people who belong to it. How dedicated we are is how dedicated our church is going to be. We have a responsibility. We are bought with a price.

Where do you live? In *Philippians 1:21* or *Philippians 2:21*? Where did Phebe live? There is no question that she lived in *Philippians 1:21, "For me to live is Christ, and to die is gain."*

STRENGTHENING GOD'S PEOPLE

Chapter Five

Romans 16:1, 2, "I commend unto you Phebe our sister, which is a servant of the church which is at Cenchrea: That ye receive her in the Lord, as becometh saints, and that ye assist her in whatsoever business she hath need of you: for she hath been a succourer of many, and of myself also."

When Paul said of Phebe that she *"hath been a succourer of many, and of myself also,"* he was talking about her helping God's people. To succour means to come to the aid of or strengthen others. That is what the Lord wants us to do, strengthen others. But we cannot do that unless we have been strengthened.

In *Hebrews 2:18* the Word of God says of Christ, *"...He is able to succour them that are tempted."* Phebe was not only a strong Christian herself, but she was able to strengthen other believers as well. What a blessing she was to others.

In a day when so many of God's people are battling the world, the flesh, and the devil, we need a ministry in the local church dedicated to strengthening God's people. The church needs strong ladies who know how to strengthen others. Every church needs ladies to be the Christians that the Lord wants them to be.

Rome was not an easy place to live for the Lord. Paul said that he was ready for Rome in *Romans 1:15*: *"So, as much as in me is, I am ready to preach the gospel to you that are at Rome also."* Phebe was sent to Rome because she was ready. Paul could not have sent just any Christian to Rome; they would not have been able to handle it. But Phebe was ready to go because she was a strong Christian lady. Phebe understood the challenge of the world and knew how to help other believers become overcomers.

The day in which we live is much like Rome. We need to be ready. We must be strong Christians if we are going to make a difference in the lives of people. One of our church's mottoes is "Making a difference in the lives of people." It is from *Jude 1:22, "And of some have compassion, making a difference."*

What does the Lord use to strengthen His people? What makes a strong Christian? There are five things that every Christian lady can do to be strengthened. If ladies will do these five things, they will become strong in the Lord and will possess the ability to strengthen others.

The five things that strengthen God's people are covered in this lesson. Each one is illustrated with a tree representing the fruit that is produced as a result of doing each one. If one of these five things is neglected, the fruit that would have been produced is missing in the believer's life.

The five things that every believer must do to be strengthened are as follows.

Spend Time Every Day in God's Word

First, we should read the Bible every day. *Acts 17:11* says, *"These were more noble than those in Thessalonica, in that they received the Word with all readiness of mind, and searched the scriptures daily, whether those things were so."* Notice that they had *"readiness of mind"* and they *"searched the scriptures daily."* These are the key words in this verse.

Sometimes when I read my Bible, I have many things on my mind. That is why the Bible tells us to spend time with the Lord early in the morning. This is a good time because we are just waking up and we do not have so much on our minds. We can be awake for only an hour and already the busyness starts creeping in. We think about all that we need to do. We must have readiness of mind when we read our Bibles and pray every day so that God can speak to us.

When I read and pray for any length of time, my mind can start to wander. We need to keep our minds under subjection. *II Corinthians 10:5* says, *"Casting down imaginations, and every high thing that exalteth itself against the knowledge of God, and bringing into captivity every thought to the obedience of Christ."* We must guard our thoughts because the devil tries to steal our concentration from us. Have readiness of mind and search the Scriptures daily.

Psalm 119:165 says, *"Great peace have they which love Thy law; and nothing shall offend them."* Dr. Lee Roberson gives the illustration

of complimenting a person in a grave and getting no reaction because that person is dead. If the person in the grave is insulted and ridiculed, the reaction is the same: nothing. They are dead. We need to die to self. We do not need to take everything so personally. Shrug it off and laugh about it. This helps us to get over things.

Spending time in God's Word daily will produce fruit in the believer's life.

Faith in the Lord.

Spending time in God's Word will produce faith in the Lord. Faith is claiming God's promises. *"Now faith is the substance of things hoped for, the evidence of things not seen" (Hebrews 11:1).*

It takes faith to please God. *Hebrews 11:6* says, *"But without faith it is impossible to please Him…"* The goal of the Christian life is to please God. The Lord Jesus said in *John 8:29*, *"…I do always those things that please Him."*

We need to have faith in the Lord. As we spend time in God's Word, we need to ask the Lord to increase our faith. *Romans 10:17* says, *"So then faith cometh by hearing, and hearing by the Word of God."* The more time we spend in God's Word and meditating on God's Word, the more our faith increases. We cannot grow in faith and ignore God's Word.

Direction for life.

Spending time in God's Word will give us direction for life. God will never lead us contrary to the teaching of His Word. If we are praying about a matter and seeking counsel to make a decision, the answer will be according to God's Word. God will never guide us opposite from His Word. That is a great truth that we can trust.

Psalm 119:105 says, *"Thy Word is a lamp unto my feet, and a light unto my path."* God will show us the next step through His Word. He is not going to reveal everything to us at once. We think we would like Him to give us a detailed diagram of what comes next, but that is not the way the Lord works. We have to take one step at a time. We take a step and He shows us the next step. We take another step and He shows us the next. If we do not take that step, He is not going to show us any more. When God shows us light, we need to walk in that light. If we do not, He will not show us any more. He will give us direction, but He will show us one step at a time.

Psalm 143:8 is a prayer: *"Cause me to hear Thy lovingkindness in the morning; for in Thee do I trust: cause me to know the way wherein I should walk; for I lift up my soul unto Thee."* (Notice this verse says *"in the morning"* when our minds are fresher.) God will cause us to know the way if we get into the Bible and read God's Word.

Understanding in the working of the Lord.

Spending time in God's Word will produce understanding in the working of the Lord. *Psalm 119:100* and *104* say, *"I understand more than the ancients, because I keep Thy precepts...Through Thy precepts I get understanding: therefore I hate every false way."*

We can measure the maturity of a person by how they understand. *I Corinthians 13:11* says, *"When I was a child, I spake as a child, I understood as a child, I thought as a child: but when I became a man, I put away childish things."* We cannot take people any further than they are willing to go. We can measure the maturity of a Christian by how they understand. It is revealing.

Understanding the working of the Lord is like God turning on the light. We can be reading our Bibles and all of a sudden one word or sentence

comes alive. We can read the same Scripture several times and every time get something new out of it. That is the way the Lord works. Understanding the working of the Lord is something we need to strive for.

Deliverance from personal battles.

We can get deliverance from personal battles if we will spend time in God's Word. *Psalm 107:20* says, *"He sent His Word, and healed them, and delivered them from their destructions."* This is a great verse. We need deliverance from personal battles. *John 8:32* says, *"And ye shall know the truth, and the truth shall make you free."*

God's Word has the power to make us new people. It begins with our thought life, and then we are transformed according to *Romans 12:2: "And be not conformed to this world: but be ye **transformed by the renewing of your mind**, that ye may prove what is that good, and acceptable, and perfect, will of God."* People need to have their thinking changed if they are going to act differently. *Philippians 2:5* says, *"Let this mind be in you, which was also in Christ Jesus."*

Spiritual growth.

If we spend time every day in God's Word, we will grow spiritually. *II Peter 3:18* says, *"But grow in grace, and in the knowledge of our Lord and Saviour Jesus Christ..."* If we want to grow, we have to get into the Bible. We are not going to grow if we do not read our Bibles. *"As newborn babes, desire the sincere milk of the Word, that ye may grow thereby"* (*I Peter 2:2*).

A good test to see if we are growing spiritually is to gauge how we react to the pressures and difficulties of life. *II Peter 1:5* and *6* say, *"And*

beside this, giving all diligence, add to your faith…temperance…"
Temperance is self-control. Being able to handle what the world throws at us is temperance.

Ladies who spend time in God's Word will have this fruit. Ladies who neglect God's Word will experience lack.

The following tree illustrates what daily Bible reading produces in the believer's life. Spending time in God's Word will give us this fruit:

Faith. Do you have faith? Is your faith increasing?
Direction. Are you getting direction in your life?
Understanding. Is God giving you understanding?
Deliverance. Have you experienced deliverance from
             personal battles?
Spiritual Growth. Are you growing spiritually?

If any of these fruits are missing in your life, then you are neglecting the Bible. This tree is a good illustration because it shows the root of this fruit is daily Bible reading. Make sure you read your Bible every day.

Do you want to deal with the fruit of the problem or the root of the problem? Many people are dealing with the fruit. People sometimes complicate things, but the Lord Jesus makes things very simple. If you are missing any of these fruits, there is one problem. You are missing the root, daily Bible reading. It is very simple. You cannot have the fruit without the root.

GOD'S WORD

Understanding

Direction

Deliverance

Faith

Spiritual Growth

DailyBibleReading

Romans 10:17 - *Faith in the Lord*

Psalm 119:105, Psalm 143:8 - *Direction for Life*

Psalm 119:100, 104 - *Understanding in the Working of the Lord*

Psalm 107:20 - *Deliverance from Personal Battles*

II Peter 3:8 - *Spiritual Growth*

Develop a Personal Prayer Life

Second, we need to develop a personal prayer life. I love this verse. In *Jeremiah 33:3* God says, *"Call unto Me, and I will answer thee, and shew thee great and mighty things, which thou knowest not."* There are a lot of things we do not know. God can show us so many things if we will just pray and ask Him.

Matthew 7:7 and *8* say, *"Ask, and it shall be given you; seek, and ye shall find; knock, and it shall be opened unto you: For every one that asketh receiveth; and he that seeketh findeth; and to him that knocketh it shall be opened."* Spending time daily in prayer will produce the following fruit:

Victory and spiritual growth in the lives of others.

Prayer produces victory. If we pray for people, they will win personal victories. We have a responsibility as Christians. We are bought with a price. *"For ye are bought with a price: therefore glorify God in your body, and in your spirit, which are God's" (I Corinthians 6:20).*

We need to be right just so we can pray. *James 5:16* says, *"The effectual fervent prayer of a **righteous** man availeth much."*

A lady asked me to pray for her and her children because she could not pray for them herself. She said she was not on praying ground. How sad. That is one thing I want in my life: to be able to pray for my family and for others. Her words stung me and surprised me.

We all need to be on praying ground. It is important. Not only do *we* need the Lord's help, but *others* do also, not just our family members, but also the world. Who will pray for them if we do not? We can win victory and spiritual growth in the lives of others.

Colossians 1:9 says, *"For this cause we also, since the day we heard it, do not cease to pray for you, and to desire that ye might be filled with the knowledge of His will in all wisdom and spiritual understanding."* Who have you prayed for that God has blessed?

I Timothy 2:1 says, *"I exhort therefore, that, first of all, supplications, prayers, intercessions, and giving of thanks, be made for all men."* The Bible commands us to pray for others. We will never know the power of prayer if we do not have a personal devotional life.

In *Acts 12:1-19* we read that Peter was put in prison and was going to be killed. *Acts 12:5* tells us, *"Peter therefore was kept in prison: but prayer was made without ceasing of the church unto God for him."* Later in verse *17* Peter *"...declared unto them how the Lord had brought him out of the prison..."* God's people prayed for Peter and he was delivered.

Think of our missionaries who would be saddened to know that no one is praying for them. They have many difficulties on the mission field. They need our prayers. We have a responsibility to pray for them as they labor on foreign soil.

The blessing of God on our lives.

If we develop a personal prayer life, we will receive the blessing of God on our lives. *Jeremiah 33:3* says, *"Call unto Me, and I will answer thee, and shew thee great and mighty things, which thou knowest not."*

James 4:2 says, *"Ye lust, and have not: ye kill, and desire to have, and cannot obtain: ye fight and war, yet ye have not, because ye ask not."* That is simple. The Lord does not mean that we will have everything we *want*, but rather everything we *need* for which we pray. If we ask Him, He will give it to us. I think we all agree that we have not because we ask not. We must learn how to want our needs and not need our wants.

A closeness to the Lord.

A personal prayer life will bring a closeness to the Lord. *James 4:8* says, *"Draw nigh to God, and He will draw nigh to you..."* This great verse teaches that if we take a step toward the Lord, He takes a step toward us. We must realize that if we desire to be closer to the Lord, it is our move first.

We are close to the people we talk to. The more we talk, the closer we are. The more we talk to the Lord, the closer our relationship will become with Him. He is the *"friend that sticketh closer than a brother"* *(Proverbs 18:24)*.

Power in the preaching and teaching of God's Word.

If we develop a personal prayer life, we will have power in the preaching and teaching of God's Word. *II Thessalonians 3:1* says, *"Finally, brethren, pray for us, that the Word of the Lord may have free course, and be glorified, even as it is with you."*

My husband often speaks of Goldie Brown. She prayed for her preacher and it made a big difference. We need to pray for power for our pastor and Sunday school teachers as they preach and teach God's Word.

When we teach the Bible, we need to pray. It is not easy to get up and teach the Bible. There is always the fear that something will be said that should not be said. I always pray that the Lord will let me say what He wants me to say and take away what I should not say.

Witnessing is teaching. In *Matthew 28:19* the Lord Jesus said, *"Go ye therefore, and teach all nations…"* Teach people how to be saved. We need to pray for power as the gospel is given. *"And when they had **prayed**, the place was shaken where they were assembled together; and they were all filled with the Holy Ghost, and they spake the Word of God with boldness…And with great **power** gave the apostles witness…" (Acts 4:31, 33).*

We need to pray for power in the preaching and teaching of God's Word. God's Word is powerful. *Psalm 107:20* says, *"He sent His Word, and healed them, and delivered them from their destructions."* The Lord uses us as tools, so we need to be right. The Word of God would have more effect on the lives of people if we prayed for the ones who are teaching and preaching God's Word.

Defense against the devil.

If we develop a personal prayer life, we will have a defense against the devil. *Ephesians 6:18* says, *"Praying always with all prayer and supplication in the Spirit, and watching thereunto with all perseverance and supplication for all saints."*

The Lord Jesus told Peter that Satan wanted to destroy him, but He also told Peter that He prayed for him: *"And the Lord said, Simon, Simon, behold, Satan hath desired to have you, that he may sift you as wheat: But I have prayed for thee, that thy faith fail not: and when thou art converted, strengthen thy brethren" (Luke 22:31, 32).* The Lord's prayer protected Peter.

In *Acts 12:12-17* God's people prayed for Peter for deliverance, and he was delivered out of the hand of the enemy. How many people would be delivered if we would just pray for them? There are many people in our church who need our prayers. They can be delivered if we pray for them.

Romans 8:26 says, *"Likewise the Spirit also helpeth our infirmities: for we know not what we should pray for as we ought: but the Spirit itself maketh intercession for us with groanings which cannot be uttered."* Sometimes we pray without even knowing what to say. We are just trying to communicate with the Lord. The Holy Spirit comes along and helps us. We can even pray amiss, and the Lord will still bless us because He knows our hearts. We should ask the Holy Spirit to lead us in our requests to God. The Holy Spirit will impress on our minds and hearts what to say.

We need to have a daily prayer list and get serious about it. One day we will see how much we really prayed and cared for people. When I think how little I have prayed for people and for the work of the Lord, I am ashamed. We can begin today to fill our lives and time with prayer.

Rewards in Heaven.

Developing a personal prayer life gives us rewards in Heaven. *Revelation 5:8* says, *"And when He had taken the book, the four beasts and four and twenty elders fell down before the Lamb, having every one of them harps, and golden vials full of odours, which are the prayers of saints."* Our prayers are in vials.

Revelation 8:3 and *4* say, *"And another angel came and stood at the altar, having a golden censer; and there was given unto him much incense, that he should offer it with the prayers of all saints upon the golden altar which was before the throne. And the smoke of the*

incense, which came with the prayers of the saints, ascended up before God out of the angel's hand."

Our prayers are being kept in golden vials and will one day be offered to God as a testimony to how much we loved the Lord Jesus and how He blessed and cared for us. Will we rejoice when we see our prayers offered to the Lord?

Ladies who spend time in prayer will have these fruits in their lives. Ladies who do not develop a personal prayer life will lack in these areas.

Following is the tree of prayer. The root is prayer. If we have a prayer life, it will produce:

✦ **Victory and spiritual growth.**
✦ **The blessing of God.**
✦ **Closeness to the Lord.**
✦ **Power in preaching and teaching.**
✦ **Defense against the devil.**
✦ **Rewards in Heaven.**

Do you have these fruits in your life? If you are missing any of these fruits, there is a problem with the root. The root is prayer. We must remember that to produce the fruit, we must have the root.

PRAYER

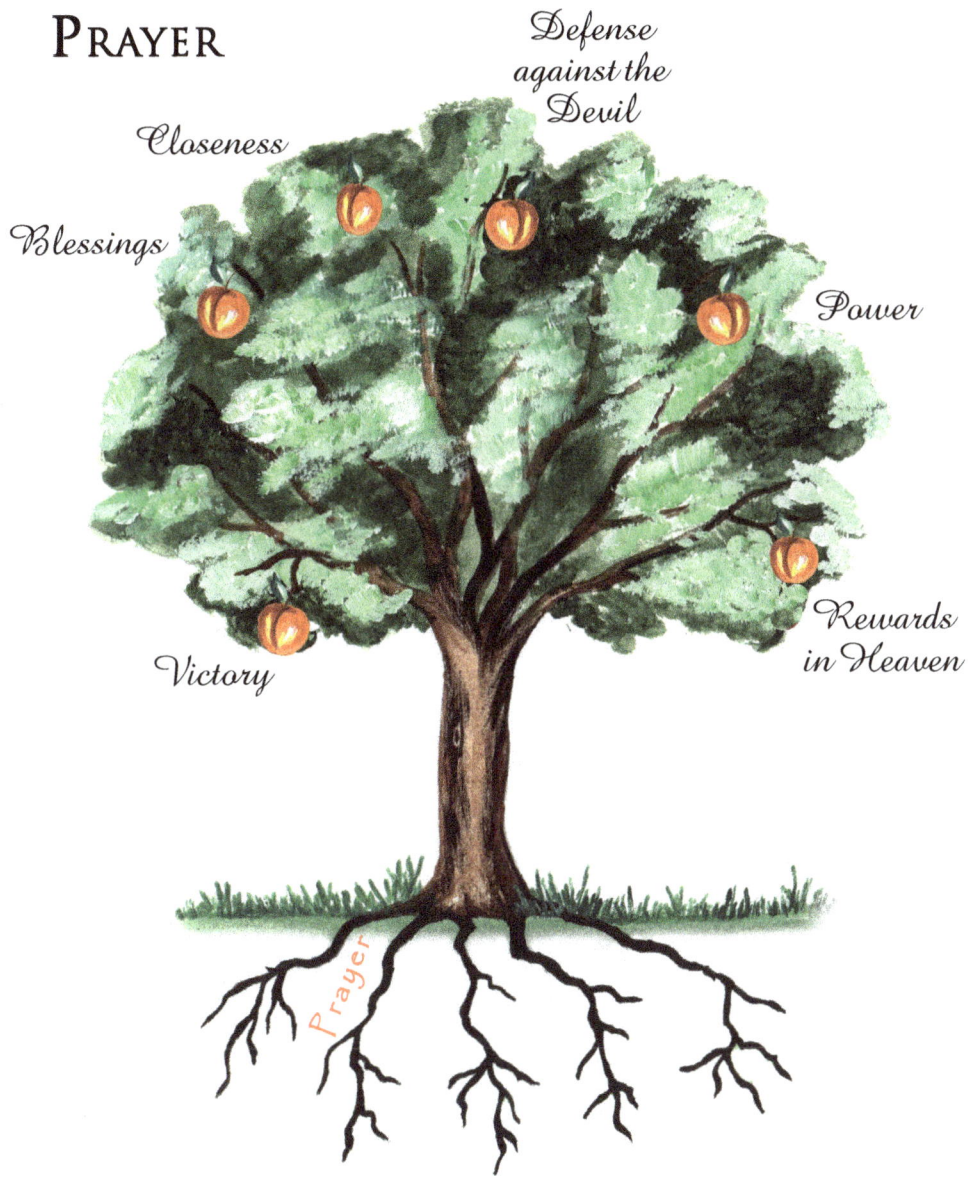

Defense
against the
Devil

Closeness

Blessings

Power

Victory

Rewards
in Heaven

Prayer

Colossians 1:9, I Timothy 2:1 - *Victory and Spiritual Growth in the Lives of Others*

Jeremiah 33:3, James 4:2 - *The Blessing of God on Our Lives*

James 4:8 - *A Closeness to the Lord*

II Thessalonians 3:1 - *Power in the Preaching and Teaching of God's Word*

Ephesians 6:18, Romans 8:26 - *Defense Against the Devil*

Revelation 5:8, Revelation 8:3,4 - *Rewards in Heaven*

Faithfulness to Church

Third, we must be faithful to church. *Hebrews 10:24* and *25* say, *"And let us consider one another to provoke unto love and to good works: Not forsaking the assembling of ourselves together, as the manner of some is; but exhorting one another: and so much the more, as ye see the day approaching."*

Psalm 92:13 says, *"Those that be planted in the house of the LORD shall flourish in the courts of our God."*

These verses make it plain that God wants us in church.

*"Those that be **planted** in the house of the LORD shall flourish…"* Faithfulness to church produces a *planted* Christian. There is a difference between being a *planted* Christian and being a *potted* Christian. When a plant is in a pot, it can be taken out. There is no permanence. There is no room to grow either. Pot-bound plants do not flourish; their roots are too crowded in the pot.

I have always wanted to grow roses so I bought some rose bushes. I had about six of them, all different colors, all so beautiful, all on my porch in a pot. They were blooming and I was babying them and having a great time. My husband said, "You are going to have to get them out of the pot or they are going to die." I said, "No, I don't want to," because I was afraid they *would* die if *I* did anything to them—that is how I am with plants. But I took them out of the pot anyway and planted them in the yard. That was the only hope for them. The only chance they had to live and grow was to be planted.

Normally when something is planted it takes root. Those roots grow into the ground deeper and deeper and deeper. The plant flourishes. That is what this verse is talking about. We must plant ourselves in the house of the Lord and then we will flourish. Our roots will grow deeper and deeper and we will become stronger and stronger. If we put our roots down in a good church the Lord will bless our lives.

Encouragement in the life of the child of God.

Faithfulness to church produces encouragement in the believer's life. *Hebrews 10:25* says, *"Not forsaking the assembling of ourselves together, as the manner of some is; but exhorting one another: and so much the more, as ye see the day approaching."*

We need to exhort one another daily. We need to pray for and encourage each other. *Hebrews 3:13* says, *"But exhort one another daily, while it is called To day; lest any of you be hardened through the deceitfulness of sin."*

The opposite of encouragement is discouragement. When people begin to miss church services, they become discouraged. Often they do not even realize what caused their discouragement. I have never met a Christian who was unfaithful to church who was not discouraged.

Fellowship with God's people.

Faithfulness to church produces fellowship with God's people. Church is a fellowship of baptized believers. Fellowship is one of the glues that hold a church together. It is a spirit of one accord.

We cannot have fellowship with someone if we are not in one accord with them. *I John 1:7* says, *"But if we walk in the light, as He is in the light, we have **fellowship** one with another, and the blood of Jesus*

Christ His Son cleanseth us from all sin." How can we have fellowship with one another if we are not walking in the same light?

Ladies whose husbands are not saved have such difficulty because they are not walking in the same light and it is hard for them to have fellowship. They cannot have the kind of fellowship the Lord wants them to have. It is the same with ladies who have unsaved family members or friends.

Acts 2:42 says, *"And they continued stedfastly in the apostles' doctrine and **fellowship**, and in breaking of bread, and in prayers."* We need fellowship with other Christians and that need is met in the church.

Protection from the world, the flesh, and the devil.

Job 1:10 says, *"Hast not Thou made an hedge about him, and about his house, and about all that he hath on every side? Thou hast blessed the work of his hands, and his substance is increased in the land."*

In *Proverbs 10:8* we read, *"The wise in heart will receive commandments: but a prating fool shall fall."* If we have a closed heart and mind, we are going to fall, and we are fools. But if we have a wise heart, we will receive the things of the Lord.

In *Luke 22:32*, the Lord Jesus told Simon Peter, *"But I have prayed for thee…"* There is protection in God's family. The safest place for our families is in a strong church. Many families have been devoured because they left a good church. A strong church is the safest place we can be.

Asaph said that he did not fully understand the destruction and power of the world, the flesh, and the devil until he went to the house of God. *"Until I went into the sanctuary of God; then understood I their end" (Psalm 73:17).*

Opportunity to have a part in the Lord's work.

Faithfulness to the local church produces opportunity to have a part in the Lord's work. *II Timothy 2:2* says, *"And the things that thou hast heard of me among many witnesses, the same commit thou to faithful men, who shall be able to teach others also."* This verse is talking about faithful men being witnesses and having an opportunity to be a part of the Lord's work.

We have to be faithful in order to be a part of the Lord's work. Faithful people in church have an opportunity to teach others. God is not going to use people to teach others unless they are faithful. It sometimes amazes me who Christians go to for advice. We should never ask advice of a lost person or someone who is not faithful.

Revelation 2:8-10 says, *"And unto the angel of the church in Smyrna write; These things saith the first and the last, which was dead, and is alive; I know thy works, and tribulation, and poverty, (but thou art rich) and I know the blasphemy of them which say they are Jews, and are not, but are the synagogue of Satan. Fear none of those things which thou shalt suffer: behold, the devil shall cast some of you into prison, that ye may be tried; and ye shall have tribulation ten days:* **be thou faithful unto death, and I will give thee a crown of life."** God wants us to be faithful.

The joy of the Lord.

Church has a rejoicing spirit. Have you ever been really "down", but coming to church picked you up? That is the Lord giving you joy. *Acts 8:8* says, *"And there was great joy in that city."*

Acts 2:46 says, *"And they, continuing daily with one accord in the temple, and breaking bread from house to house, did eat their meat with gladness and singleness of heart."* The happiest people in the world are God's people. The joy of the Lord is still our strength. *Nehemiah 8:10* tells us *"the joy of the LORD is your strength."*

Look at the fruit on the next tree. Ladies who are faithful to church will have this fruit. Ladies who neglect being faithful to church will experience lack in these areas.

Faithfulness to church produces:

✦ **Encouragement for the Christian life.**
✦ **Fellowship with God's people.**
✦ **Protection from the world, the flesh, and the devil.**
✦ **Opportunity for Christian service.**
✦ **Joy in the believer's life.**

If any of this fruit is missing in your life, check the root of it, which is faithfulness to church. If you want the fruit, you have to have the root.

FAITHFULNESS TO CHURCH

Protection

Fellowship

Opportunity

Joy

Encouragement

Church

Hebrews 10:25 - *Encouragement in the Life of the Child of God*

I John 1:7, Acts 2:42 - *Fellowship with God's People*

Job 1:10, Proverbs 10:8, Luke 22:32 - *Protection from the World, the Flesh and the Devil*

II Timothy 2:2 - *Opportunity to Have a Part in the Lord's Work*

Acts 8:8, Acts 2:46 - *Joy of the Lord*

Faithfulness in Giving

Fourth, we must be faithful in giving. Do not try to figure giving out on paper. It will not work. It is a matter of faith. If we try to figure our budgets out on paper and how we are going to give to the Lord, it will not add up. We must give by faith.

When my husband was in college, he was working nights, and we were putting our children through Christian school. We tithed faithfully every week and there were some weeks I thought we were not going to be able to buy groceries, but the Lord always blessed us. God always provided for us one way or another.

God knows how to provide for His children, but we have to test Him. God says, *"Bring ye all the tithes into the storehouse ... and **prove Me** ... if I will not open you the windows of heaven, and pour you out a blessing ... "* *(Malachi 3:10)*. We have to take that step of faith in our giving.

Too many people hit and miss at giving. They try and they quit. It is like taking medicine. The doctor says, "Take the whole bottle." Sometimes we think, "Oh, I don't need this anymore," so we quit taking it, and then we have a relapse. We should know better. Neither can we hit and miss at giving. We have to be faithful, because God is not going to be faithful to us unless we are faithful to Him.

I Corinthians 4:2 says, *"Moreover it is required in stewards, that a man be found faithful."* *II Corinthians 8:3* says, *"For to their power, I bear record, yea, and beyond their power they were willing of themselves."*

We have to be faithful in giving long enough for it to take root. We have to be faithful to the Lord. It takes time to take root. Things do not always happen overnight with the Lord. It is always in His timing, and His timing is never our timing. We have to wait on the Lord, which is probably the hardest thing to do. But if we are faithful to Him, He will be faithful to us. He will prove Himself. He says, "Prove Me." That means, "Test Me. Try Me."

Giving produces fruit in our lives. It produces:

The windows of Heaven opened in our lives.

If we are faithful in giving, the windows of Heaven open in our lives. *Malachi 3:10* says, *"Bring ye all the tithes into the storehouse, that there may be meat in Mine house, and prove Me now herewith, saith the LORD of hosts, if I will not open you the windows of heaven, and pour you out a blessing, that there shall not be room enough to receive it."* The Lord is asking us to give Him an opportunity to do something in our lives, and we need to give it to Him. We need to prove Him.

Do *you* have the window of Heaven open in *your* life? God sends blessings through that window. If you have the window open a tiny crack, that is how little the Lord can bless you. If you have the window open wide, the Lord can bless you so much more. You decide how much to open the window of giving through which the Lord can bless you.

Defense against the devil.

Faithfulness in giving produces a defense against the devil. When we give, the Lord rebukes the devourer. In *Malachi 3:11*, the Lord says, *"And I will rebuke the devourer for your sakes, and he shall not destroy the fruits of your ground..."*

The devil is like a roaring lion seeking whom he may devour. *I Peter 5:8* says, *"Be sober, be vigilant; because your adversary the devil, as*

a roaring lion, walketh about, seeking whom he may devour." And he does not go to bed and take a rest either. He is on the prowl twenty-four hours a day.

The question is, do we believe the devil is real? We say we do, but do we really act like it? Do we really believe that the devil is walking around trying to devour us and our families? If we did, we would be on our faces praying more. We would not leave the house without praying to the Lord if we really believed he is our enemy. We would be obeying the Lord in tithes and offerings. Giving provides defense against the devil and we need it.

Protection of our fruit.

Faithfulness in giving will produce protection of our fruit. *Malachi 3:11* continues, *"...Neither shall your vine cast her fruit before the time in the field, saith the LORD of hosts."* The question is, what is the fruit of our lives? It is what we have accomplished in our lives, our families, our work, our ministry, our testimonies. All these are the fruits of our lives, and if we faithfully give, the Lord says He will protect our fruit. It would be a very unwise farmer who did not protect his fruit.

The blessings from others on our lives.

Faithfulness in giving produces the blessing from others on our lives. When we give, the Lord causes others to be a blessing to us. He says in *Luke 6:38, "Give, and it shall be given unto you; good measure, pressed down, and shaken together, and running over, shall men give into your bosom. For with the same measure that ye mete withal it shall be measured to you again."*

How many times do we get blessings because the Lord laid it on someone's heart to bless us? That has happened so many times to me and my husband and family.

It is a blessing that you do not expect. It comes as a surprise. God will put in the hearts of others to give unto you if you are a faithful giver.

Treasures in Heaven.

When we are faithful in giving, it produces treasures in Heaven. *Matthew 6:20* and *21* say, *"But lay up for yourselves treasures in heaven, where neither moth nor rust doth corrupt, and where thieves do not break through nor steal. For where your treasure is, there will your heart be also."* The Lord says that where our treasure is, our heart is.

Matthew 10:42 says, *"And whosoever shall give to drink unto one of these little ones a cup of cold water only in the name of a disciple, verily I say unto you, he shall in no wise lose his reward."* God will bless us for giving even a cup of water to a little one.

I Peter 1:4 says, *"To an inheritance incorruptible, and undefiled, and that fadeth not away, reserved in heaven for you."* We will have treasures in Heaven if we give.

What we give can be used to reach others with the gospel and provide an opportunity for the Lord to work. I like the expression that I heard years ago that says, "I'm giving while I'm living so I'm knowing where it's going."

Next we see the tree of giving. Ladies who are faithful in tithing and giving will have this fruit. Women who are not faithful with tithes and offerings will experience lack in these areas. Remember: No root, no fruit.

Look at the tree of giving. This is what faithfulness in giving produces.

- ✦ **Windows of Heaven opened.**
- ✦ **Defense against the devil.**
- ✦ **Protection of our fruit.**
- ✦ **Blessings from others.**
- ✦ **Treasures in Heaven.**

Look at all the fruit we get if we are just faithful in giving to the Lord.

GIVING

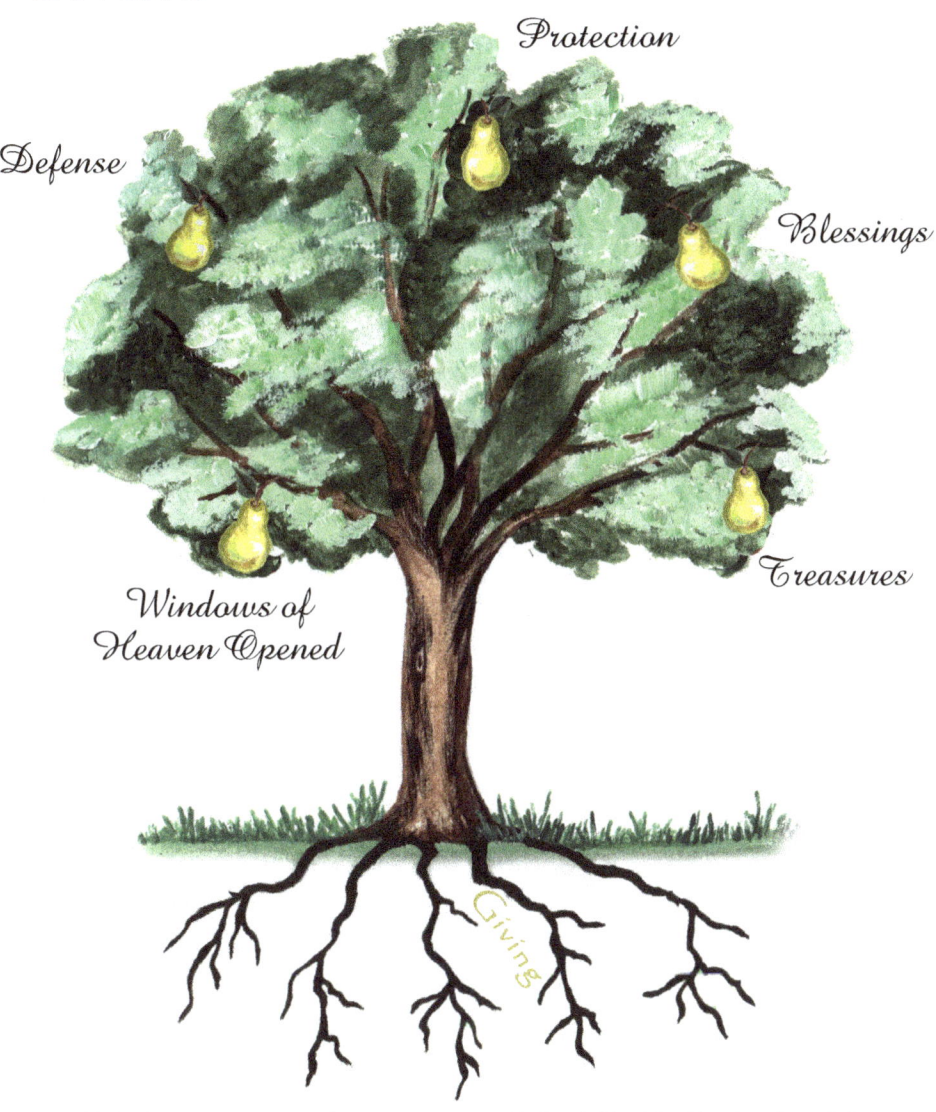

Protection

Defense

Blessings

Treasures

Windows of
Heaven Opened

Giving

Malachi 3:10 - *The Windows of Heaven Opened in Our Lives*

Malachi 3:11, 1 Peter 5:8 - *Defense Against the Devil*

Malachi 3:11 - *Protection of Our Fruit*

Luke 6:38 - *The Blessing from Others on Our Lives*

Matthew 6:20, Matthew 10:42, 1 Peter 1:4 - *Treasures in Heaven*

Faithfulness in Witnessing

Fifth, we must be faithful in witnessing. This is the one area in which we fail the most. In *Acts 1:8*, the Lord Jesus said, *"But ye shall receive power, after that the Holy Ghost is come upon you: and ye shall be witnesses unto Me both in Jerusalem, and in all Judaea, and in Samaria, and unto the uttermost part of the earth."*

Everyone who gets saved is a result of someone's witness. People cannot get saved without our witness. That is why the Bible emphasizes witnessing so much that it tells of blood dripping from our hands if we do not witness. In *Ezekiel 3:17* and *18* God says, *"Son of man, I have made thee a watchman unto the house of Israel: therefore hear the word at My mouth, and give them warning from Me. When I say unto the wicked, Thou shalt surely die; and thou givest him not warning, nor speakest to warn the wicked from his wicked way, to save his life; the same wicked man shall die in his iniquity; but his blood will I require at thine hand."*

How important it is to be a faithful witness! It is a big responsibility on our part. We need to be faithful to the Lord in witnessing. Witnessing produces fruit in a believer's life.

Joy in Heaven.

Witnessing produces joy in Heaven. *Luke 15:10* says, *"Likewise, I say unto you, there is joy in the presence of the angels of God over one sinner that repenteth."* When one sinner repents, the angels rejoice in Heaven.

Adults and children get saved all the time in our church, and sometimes we take it for granted. Some Christians have a hard time believing children can get saved, but children are very smart. My granddaughters are four and five years old, and what they have learned amazes me. I was surprised by what they knew when they were even younger. They knew Bible verses by heart already. In our church ministry, preschoolers learn scores of Bible verses before they even learn to read. These verses help prepare their hearts to receive Christ when they understand the gospel. *"And that from a child thou hast known the holy scriptures, which are able to make thee wise unto salvation through faith which is in Christ Jesus" (II Timothy 3:15).*

"...There is joy...over one sinner that repenteth." It is important to be happy when a sinner gets saved. We should rejoice. Ladies who have not had a part in someone's salvation have never really experienced the joy of the Lord.

Rewards at the Judgment Seat of Christ.

Witnessing produces rewards at the Judgment Seat of Christ. *Daniel 12:3* says, *"And they that be wise shall shine as the brightness of the firmament; and they that turn many to righteousness as the stars for ever and ever."* This verse is referring to soul winners shining like stars forever.

Proverbs 11:30 says, *"The fruit of the righteous is a tree of life; and he that winneth souls is wise."* We all want to be wise. We all want wisdom from the Lord, so we all need to win souls.

Imagine what it is like when a faithful witness arrives in Heaven. There are people rejoicing to see the one who led them to the Lord. There will be rewards at the Judgment Seat of Christ. There is a great cloud of witnesses in Heaven rejoicing over a race run well. *Hebrews 12: 1 and 2* say, *"Wherefore seeing we also are compassed about with so great a*

cloud of witnesses, let us lay aside every weight, and the sin which doth so easily beset us, and let us run with patience the race that is set before us, Looking unto Jesus…"

Compassion in a believer's life.

In *Matthew 9:35* and *36*, the Bible says, *"And Jesus went about all the cities and villages, teaching in their synagogues, and preaching the gospel of the kingdom, and healing every sickness and every disease among the people. But when He saw the multitudes, He was moved with compassion on them, because they fainted, and were scattered abroad, as sheep having no shepherd."* Seeing the multitudes of people moved the Lord; He had compassion on them. Seeing people where they are changes our hearts.

We do not get compassion by thinking about it or praying about it. Compassion comes when we go and witness. *"Jesus went…He saw the multitudes,"* and *"He was moved with compassion on them."*

The biggest lessons I ever learned were learned on my bus route. If we ever become cold-hearted, we should go out on a Saturday morning and visit on someone's bus route. It will bring us right back to where we need to be. If we think we have problems, we need to go see people where they live. We all have problems, things that we deal with every day, heartaches, burdens we are bearing; but when we go out witnessing or visiting, and we see people, it puts it all in perspective. Children love to come to church and love the Lord, and when we visit their homes and see what these poor children have to live in, it really gets our priorities and thinking straight. All our problems seem to disappear. We think we have problems but they are nothing like what these poor children have to face.

We get compassion by getting out there and being among people. That is the only way to get compassion. Compassion changes people's lives.

Vision for the work of the Lord.

Faithfulness in witnessing produces vision for the work of the Lord. *Matthew 9:37* and *38* say, *"Then saith He unto His disciples, The harvest truly is plenteous, but the labourers are few; Pray ye therefore the Lord of the harvest, that He will send forth labourers into His harvest."* It is sad that the labourers are few. If every single person who attends this church was a soul winner, think of all the people who would be going to Heaven. We need to be faithful witnesses.

Proverbs 29:18 tells us, *"Where there is no vision, the people perish; but he that keepeth the law, happy is he."* I thank God that my husband had a vision for this place. This church is a real testimony.

My husband had a vision for Cape Coral years ago. When we were first saved, we left here to go to Bible college, and he used to urge everyone who graduated, "Go to Cape Coral. They really need a good church." My husband did not think of going himself for some reason, maybe because we grew up here. *"For Jesus Himself testified, that a prophet hath no honour in his own country" (John 4:44).* Finally the Lord told him *he* needed to go to Cape Coral!

"Where there is no vision, the people perish." There is a vision here. There are goals, and we all need to be witnesses and workers so these goals are carried out. Our vision is to reach the people of this city. Are you a part of the vision?

Victory in the believer's life.

Another fruit that is produced by faithfulness in witnessing is victory in the believer's life. We sing a song that I love which says, "I'm on the winning side." We can be on the winning side. We can have victory in the Lord.

I Corinthians 9:27 says, *"But I keep under my body, and bring it into subjection: lest that by any means, when I have preached to others, I myself should be a castaway."* Nothing discourages people more than a Christian who turns back. That is the worst testimony of all. There are lost people who can tell us what Christians should and should not do. They know how Christians should act though they do not act right themselves. Christians who turn back hurt other people so badly.

The Lord knows what we can handle and going through hard times strengthens us, but nothing discourages people more than a Christian turning back. Some people say it is no one's business what they do, but that is so untrue. What we do and say affects our families and friends and so many others.

We have to realize that we need victory in the Lord. We need to think about the things we do and how they influence others. It might not seem important, but Paul said, *"Wherefore, if meat make my brother to offend, I will eat no flesh while the world standeth, lest I make my brother to offend" (I Corinthians 8:13).* We may do things that are not wrong, they are not sin, but if they offend other Christians, we need to consider not doing them. If we are going to do something for the Lord with our lives, we have to think about the things we do, because people are watching us.

I am very careful about what I wear even when I clean around the house. If I am outside sweeping, I always dress appropriately. I had a neighbor in Chattanooga who came over one day and asked, "Do you always look like that? Even when you clean you always look so nice." She had been watching me. I never dreamed my neighbors were watching me. It meant something to her, and she and her family ended up getting saved and going to our church. After she got saved, she told me, "You are the best Christian that I have ever known." I thought, "How sad, because I am far from perfect."

You never know who is watching you. You are a testimony, good or bad. We all are. If we want victory to win souls and to be all we can be for the Lord, we have to be careful. *Romans 14:7 says, "For none of us liveth to himself, and no man dieth to himself."*

Look at the tree of witnessing. Faithfulness in witnessing produces:

✦ **Joy in Heaven.**
✦ **Rewards at the Judgment Seat of Christ.**
✦ **Compassion for others.**
✦ **Vision for the Lord's work.**
✦ **Victory in the Christian life.**

If you want the fruit, you have to have the root. No witnessing causes lack of this fruit.

WITNESSING

Compassion

Vision

Rewards

Joy

Victory

Witnessing

Luke 15:10 - *Joy in Heaven*

Daniel 12:3, Proverbs 11:30 - *Rewards at the Judgment Seat of Christ*

Matthew 9:35,36 - *Compassion in a Believer's Life*

Matthew 9:37,38, Proverbs 29:18 - *Vision for the Work of the Lord*

I Corinthians 9:27 - *Victory in the Believer's Life*

As we look at this last tree, look at all the fruits! It would be great if we had all those fruits in our lives. If we want all these fruits, we must have these roots:

+ **Daily Bible reading.**
+ **Prayer.**
+ **Faithfulness to church.**
+ **Giving.**
+ **Witnessing.**

Christians are made strong as a result of doing these five things, and will have weakness in their lives as a result of neglecting any of these five things. Is there any fruit missing in your life? What is the neglected root?

Anyone who wishes to strengthen God's people must be able to see and recognize the lack of fruit in a believer's life, and understand the root being neglected that causes the lack.

Understanding   Protection   Encouragement

Compassion   Closeness   Defense   Opportunity

Direction   Fellowship

Faith   Power

                                                        Joy

                                                        Vision

Victory   Rewards

Blessings   Deliverance

Windows of   Spiritual
Heaven Opened   Growth

                                                Treasures

DailyBibleReading   Prayer   Church   Giving   Witnessing

A SOUL WINNER

Chapter Six

Romans 16:1, 2, "I commend unto you Phebe our sister, which is a servant of the church which is at Cenchrea: That ye receive her in the Lord, as becometh saints, and that ye assist her in whatsoever business she hath need of you: for she hath been a succourer of many, and of myself also."

The footnote to the *Book of Romans* says, *"Written to the Romans from Corinthus, and **sent by Phebe** servant of the church at Cenchrea."*

We learn from this footnote, passed down through the centuries, that the *Book of Romans,* written by Paul under the inspiration of the Holy Spirit, was carried by the hand of Phebe to the church, which was at Rome. Phebe's character and testimony must have been of the highest level for her to be chosen and given this privilege. She held in her hand and carried to the church at Rome the *Book of Romans*.

To carry the Olympic torch is considered by many a great honor. Phebe was chosen to carry something far greater. She carried in her hand a message of hope for a lost and dying world. God honored her by recording her name in His Word. We too have been given the privilege to carry His message, and God will reward us at the Judgment Seat of Christ.

The *Book of Romans* has been used for many years to lead people to Christ. It contains what we call the "Romans Road." This is one of the first things that a Christian learns who desires to win the lost. Every church needs a group of ladies who are committed to sharing the gospel with the lost.

Phebe was without a doubt a soul winner. Ladies who are part of the Phebe Fellowship should win the lost. *Proverbs 11:30* tells us that *"he that winneth souls is wise."* What must we know in order to win the lost?

Presenting The Gospel

First, we must know how to present the gospel. *Romans 1:16* says, *"For I am not ashamed of the gospel of Christ: for it is the power of God unto salvation to every one that believeth; to the Jew first, and also to the Greek."*

Sharing with someone how to be saved is as simple as the ABCs. This is a very easy way to learn it.

"A" is for Acknowledge.

"For all have sinned, and come short of the glory of God" (Romans 3:23).

We must first acknowledge that everyone is a sinner. When we are presenting the gospel to someone we have to "get them lost" before we can "get them saved." In other words, we have to help them realize that they are a sinner. I have witnessed to some people and could not get them to admit they were sinners. If we cannot get past that point, there is nothing we can do. They have to acknowledge that they are a sinner. *"For **all** have sinned..." (Romans 3:23).*

We are all sinners. *Romans 3:10* says, *"As it is written, There is none righteous, no, not one." Romans 3:23* continues, *"For all have sinned, and come short of the glory of God."*

We are born sinners and have inherited a sinful nature. This is what we all have in common. We have to realize this.

When children realize that they are sinners, they have reached the age of accountability. Some children are very young, some are older, when they realize the difference between right and wrong. That is the age of accountability.

Some people have doubts that young children can be saved but it is plain in the Bible. In *Mark 10:14* the Lord Jesus says, *"Suffer the little children to come unto Me, and forbid them not: for of such is the kingdom of God."*

We are all born sinners. This is what we all have in common. We have inherited a sin nature. It is in our nature to do wrong. Sometimes we wonder, "Why did I do that?" We sin because we have inherited a sin nature.

Children start lying when they are so little. Their parents ask them, "Did you do that?" Before children can even talk, they will shake their heads no. Why do they do that? How do they know to lie? Why do they

not just tell the truth? That is not the way children are. This is proof that we are born sinners and have inherited a sin nature.

We are able to understand that we have inherited a sinful nature by watching children. A young child will do something wrong even when he or she has been taught to do right and obey. We are all sinners because we have inherited a sinful nature.

Romans 5:12 says, *"Wherefore, as by one man sin entered into the world, and death by sin; and so death passed upon all men, for that all have sinned."*

When we share the gospel with someone, we must help them realize that they are sinners. We have to be tactful about it because if we say, "You are a sinner," they can be offended. I always say, "The Bible says, *'For **all** have sinned, and come short of the glory of God.'"* I say, "**I** am a sinner." We start with ourselves. That softens the blow for them because some people are really sensitive about this. We cannot imagine people not thinking that they are sinners, but there are people like that. So we must be careful how we present this. I always use myself as an example.

Our choices in life prove that we are sinners. *Isaiah 53:6* says, *"All we like sheep have gone astray; we have turned every one to his own way; and the LORD hath laid on Him the iniquity of us all."*

In *James 4:17* we read, *"Therefore to him that knoweth to do good, and doeth it not, to him it is sin."* That is quite a verse. Not only are we accountable for what we do, we are also accountable for what we do *not* do. Failure to do right is just as much a sin as doing wrong.

Proverbs 20:11 says, *"Even a child is known by his doings, whether his work be pure, and whether it be right."*

The fact that we sometimes choose to do wrong is evidence that we are sinners by choice. Our actions and reactions often reveal our sinful nature.

One wrong choice makes us guilty of all. *James 2:10 says, "For whosoever shall keep the whole law, and yet offend in one point, he is guilty of all."*

In order for someone to know that they are going to Heaven they must first **acknowledge** that they are a sinner. *"For all have sinned, and come short of the glory of God" (Romans 3:23).*

"B" is for Believe.

"But God commendeth His love toward us, in that, while we were yet sinners, Christ died for us" (Romans 5:8).

"A" stands for Acknowledge. "B" stands for Believe: Believe that Jesus died for you.

Romans 5:8 says, "But God commendeth His love toward us, in that, while we were yet sinners, Christ died for us." We must believe that Jesus died for us.

Sin must be paid for. *Romans 6:23 says, "For the wages of sin is death; but the gift of God is eternal life through Jesus Christ our Lord."* The payment of sin is death. When I present the gospel, I always use the illustration of going to work and getting paid for doing the job. Likewise, there is a payment for sin.

Many people do not realize the payment of sin is death. If they did they would not live like they do. However, the payment for sin is death, and we need to make that plain to people to whom we are witnessing. *Ezekiel 18:20 says, "The soul that sinneth, it shall die…"*

There are two kinds of death. When we explain this, we have to be plain like we would for a child. That is what I always do. That is the way I like things explained to me, very simply. Sometimes people really try to complicate things.

"For the wages of sin is death..." (Romans 6:23). There are two kinds of death.

There is physical death. *Romans 5:12* says, *"Wherefore, as by one man sin entered into the world, and death by sin; and so death passed upon all men, for that all have sinned."* The first kind of death is physical death. There is another kind of death too.

There is spiritual death. *Revelation 20:14* says, *"And death and hell were cast into the lake of fire. This is the second death."* The payment of our sin is to be separated from God forever.

The Lord Jesus died for our sins. *I Corinthians 15:3* says, *"...Christ died for our sins according to the scriptures."* The Lord Jesus did not die for just one of our sins, but He died for all of our sins.

II Corinthians 5:21 says *"For He hath made Him to be sin for us, who knew no sin; that we might be made the righteousness of God in Him."* The Lord Jesus took our place on Calvary. Our sins were placed on Him. He died in our place.

The Lord Jesus was made sin for us. *"For He hath made Him to be sin for us..." (II Corinthians 5:21).*

He was separated from God. In *Matthew 27:46* the Lord Jesus cried from the cross, *"...My God, My God, why hast Thou forsaken Me?"*

He went to hell in our place. *Ephesians 4:9* says, *"...He also descended first into the lower parts of the earth."* In *Psalm 16:10* the Bible says, *"For Thou wilt not leave My soul in hell; neither wilt Thou suffer Thine Holy One to see corruption."* Jesus went to a devil's hell for us.

He rose from the grave on the third day. *I Corinthians 15:4* says, *"And that He was buried, and that He rose again the third day according to the scriptures."*

In order for someone to know that they are going to Heaven they must **believe** that Jesus died for them. *"But God commendeth His love toward us, in that, while we were yet sinners, Christ died for us"* *(Romans 5:8).*

"C" is for Call.

"For whosoever shall call upon the name of the Lord shall be saved" (Romans 10:13).

"A" stands for **Acknowledge**. "B" stands for **Believe**. "C" stands for **Call**: Call upon the Lord to save you.

We must be willing to ask or call upon the Lord to save us. *Romans 10:13* says, *"For whosoever shall call upon the name of the Lord shall be saved."* The Lord has never said "No" to anyone who has asked Him to save them.

I like to explain it like this to people. *"For whosoever..."* and I put their name in that blank. *"For* if Janet *shall call upon the name of the Lord* Janet *shall be saved."* If Janet shall call upon the name of the Lord she shall be saved. I always do that. It seems to help people.

In *Hebrews 7:25*, the Bible says, *"Wherefore He is able also to save them to the uttermost that come unto God by Him, seeing He*

ever liveth to make intercession for them. " When someone is willing to turn to Christ in repentance and faith the Lord is willing and able to save them.

Isaiah 55:6 says, *"Seek ye the LORD while He may be found, call ye upon Him while He is near."* This verse talks about the Lord speaking to someone's heart. In church services I have seen people hang onto the pew when the Holy Spirit was speaking to their hearts. If they keep resisting, He will stop speaking to them. That is a sad thing. So seek the Lord while He may be found. Call upon Him while He is near.

We must **acknowledge** that we are sinners and believe that our sin must be paid for. We must also **believe** that the Lord Jesus died for our sins, and that He is alive today, willing and able to save all those who call upon Him. Then we must be willing to **call** on Him in repentance and faith. *"For whosoever shall call upon the name of the Lord shall be saved" (Romans 10:13).*

The ABCs of Salvation

Acknowledge you are a sinner.
"For all have sinned, and come short of the glory of God"
(Romans 3:23).

Believe Jesus died for you.
"But God commendeth His love toward us, in that,
while we were yet sinners, Christ died for us" (Romans 5:8).

Call upon Him to save you.
"For whosoever shall call upon the name of the Lord
shall be saved" (Romans 10:13).

Here is an example of the sinner's prayer we can lead them in once they know and believe the ABCs of salvation. This prayer is very simple.

"Lord, I know that I am a sinner. Forgive me. Come into my heart and save me. And help me to live for You. In Jesus' name, Amen."

That is simple, is it not? Sometimes we confuse things, but that is as simple as we can get on how to lead someone to the Lord. We are talking to lost people who do not understand the things of God. So keep it very simple.

The Purpose of the Visit

Second, we need to understand the purpose of a visit. *Ezekiel 34:16* says *"I will seek that which was lost, and bring again that which was driven away, and will bind up that which was broken, and will strengthen that which was sick..."*

There are four areas that we zero in on in our visitation program. Every lady should find the area in which she believes she can be the most effective. We should all be equipped and prepared to help those in each area. This is good because we have ladies who really like to make certain kinds of visits. That is what this section covers.

Seek the lost.

"I will seek that which was lost..."

First we need to seek the lost. *"I will seek that which was lost..."* We need to make sure that everyone has a chance to hear the gospel.

Romans 10:17 says, *"So then faith cometh by hearing, and hearing by the Word of God."* Carry gospel tracts and be prepared to give a witness. Turn a tract over and lead someone to the Lord with it. We can read them word for word. That is what my husband and I did when we first got saved, and it worked and is very simple. We need to seek the lost.

Visit those who have been missing.

"...bring again that which was driven away..."

Some ladies will visit ladies who have been missing. Many ladies like to go soul winning, while some ladies also like to encourage those who have been missing to come back. We need that too, very much. *"Bring again that which was driven away."*

When people miss one Sunday it is easier to miss the second Sunday. Then it becomes a habit. That is why we should visit as soon as possible those who are missing. This is a very important part of visitation.

Encourage the brokenhearted.

"...and will bind up that which was broken..."

Some ladies will encourage the brokenhearted *"and will bind up that which was broken."* Some visits are to encourage people who are having difficulties in their lives. People who are going through the fire often feel all alone and that no one really cares for them. This is an important part of visiting too, to be an encouragement to someone.

Follow up with new Christians.

"...and will strengthen that which was sick..."

Some will follow up with new Christians. Some ladies believe that is what the Lord wants them to do. *"And will strengthen that which was sick."* We need to help and strengthen new Christians in their walk with the Lord. Make sure all new Christians are being discipled.

We should all seek to excel in all four areas but we must remember there are people who are represented in every area. They all need our help. We need to really pray about being equipped and prepared to help in each area. God may really touch your heart with one of these areas. When we come to visitation some may say "I want an encouraging visit," or "I want to follow up on a new Christian." We have all kinds of visits that need to be made.

Planning the Visitation Program

Now that we understand the purpose of visiting, we need to know about planning the visitation program.

Luke 10:1-3 says, *"After these things the Lord appointed other seventy also, and sent them **two and two** before His face into every city and place, whither He Himself would come. Therefore said He unto them, The harvest truly is great, but the labourers are few: pray ye therefore the Lord of the harvest, that He would send forth labourers into His harvest. Go your ways: behold, I send you forth as lambs among wolves."*

In *Acts 20:19* and *20* the Bible says, *"Serving the Lord with all humility of mind, and with many tears, and temptations, which befell me by the lying in wait of the Jews: And how I kept back nothing*

that was profitable unto you, but have shewed you, and have taught you publickly, and from **house to house.** *"*

These verses tell us to go visiting **two by two** and **house to house**. No ladies should ever go visiting by themselves. That is very dangerous, especially nowadays. I would be afraid just because there might be a dog! But there are other reasons we should go two by two. I could write a book on the unbelievable things that have happened to me on visitation. It is really a good idea to go two by two because we never know what might happen. Two by two, house to house.

Some questions we should consider in our visitation program are:

Who should go?

Who should go? *Matthew 28:19* and *20* tell us, *"Go ye therefore, and teach all nations, baptizing them in the name of the Father, and of the Son, and of the Holy Ghost: Teaching them to observe all things whatsoever I have commanded you: and, lo, I am with you alway, even unto the end of the world. Amen."* This means we all should go. And God says He will be with us.

I Timothy 4:12 says, *"Let no man despise thy youth; but be thou an example of the believers, in word, in conversation, in charity, in spirit, in faith, in purity."* Those who know the Lord and have a life and a testimony worth following should go.

How should we go?

How should we go? Again in *Luke10:1* we read, *"After these things the Lord appointed other seventy also, and sent them **two and two** before His face into every city and place, whither He Himself would come."* Ladies should never go visiting alone. They should always go at least two by two and, according to *Acts 20:20, "from **house to house**."* We need to go two by two and house to house. That is very simple.

We who are more experienced in soul winning and visitation should always be bringing other ladies along. We should all seek to train new ladies.

What should be avoided while on visitation and soul winning?

What should we avoid on visitation and soul winning?

We need to be careful that our visitation partner does not become our visit. We should avoid sharing personal problems and burdens with our partners while on visitation. Our conversations should be encouraging. No counseling sessions. When we go out on visitation, it is for a purpose, and we need to keep that purpose in mind. *Hebrews 3:13 says, "But exhort one another daily, while it is called To day; lest any of you be hardened through the deceitfulness of sin."* Keep the visit encouraging.

When we women get together, we like to talk. If we need to talk, we can go to lunch or something one day. Make a special time, other than on visitation. Of course we can talk in the car on the way to visits, but we must be careful not to get too involved. When I go out on visitation with ladies, we usually go over and follow up on our contacts from the last Sunday or people who missed Sunday school class, or we find new people.

We need to be careful about being too opinionated. We should avoid discussing issues with our visitation partner that are controversial like politics, news events, and personal convictions that make other people uncomfortable.

We especially need to avoid being opinionated when we are in someone's home. Some people get very upset. We must remember we are coming into their home. They are probably new Christians or not saved at all. It is a blessing if they even let us in, so we have to be careful not to talk about certain subjects. We have a purpose while on visitation and soul winning that we must keep in mind. When we leave, we should have an open door to come back.

Romans 14:19 says, *"Let us therefore follow after the things which make for peace, and things wherewith one may edify another."*

I Thessalonians 5:11 says, *"Wherefore comfort yourselves together, and edify one another, even as also ye do."*

It takes people a while to get into the shape they are in, and it will take a while for them to get out. That is what people have a hard time understanding when they get saved. They have been living without the Lord for so many years and, now that they are saved, they think their lives are going to change just like that. However, that is not the way it happens. It takes time.

> *It takes people a while to get into the shape they are in, and it will take a while for them to get out.*

We must remember this when we are trying to help people. On soul winning and visitation, we are trying to help people get to the next level, but we need to be very careful. We have some Golden Rules that we try to follow including:

✦ Accept people where they are.
✦ Never embarrass anyone.

Be careful about high-level begging. Asking someone to *pray* about a need that we hope they will *help* us with is not a prayer request but high-level begging. I know that sounds kind of crazy but we need to be careful about that. It is one thing to ask someone to pray for us and quite another to expect them to help us. *I John 3:17* says, *"But whoso hath this world's good, and* **seeth** *his brother have need, and shutteth up his bowels of compassion from him, how dwelleth the love of God in him?"* The Bible says if we *see* a brother's need, not if we *hear* a brother's need. People who are always asking others to "pray" about personal needs sometimes are only high-level begging.

Be careful about using visitation time for forced fellowship. Sometimes people get involved in the visitation program because it is the only time they can make someone fellowship with them. *I John 1:7* says, *"But if we walk in the light, as He is in the light, we have fellowship one with another, and the blood of Jesus Christ His Son cleanseth us from all sin."* The basis of our fellowship should be our willingness to walk in the light. If someone is disobedient to the clear teaching of God's Word, they will discourage others when they visit.

Be careful about venting disagreements concerning church leadership. Visitation is not the time to tell our partners all the things we disagree with about the church. It is not the time to point out all the spiritual weaknesses in other believers. This is important. Many times we go out with new Christians, their first time on visitation, and they have not been members of the church for very long. As older Christians we have to be careful what we say. We just cannot talk about things like that because they may misunderstand. *Psalm 19:14* says, *"Let the words of my mouth, and the meditation of my heart, be acceptable in Thy sight, O LORD, my strength, and my redeemer."* That is a great verse.

Matthew 7:3 says, *"And why beholdest thou the mote that is in thy brother's eye, but considerest not the beam that is in thine own eye?"* Many times we try to get the mote (a speck) out of someone else's eye when we have a beam (a log) in our own. If we will ask the Lord to help us be encouraging to other believers and to remove the things that hinder our own lives, we will not be correcting others. We need to ask the Lord to help us with *our* failures and *our* weaknesses. "There, but for the grace of God, go I." We never know when we may have to walk in someone else's shoes.

To please the Lord and to win the lost is the highest goal of the Christian life. Ladies who win others to Christ have a special place in the work of the Lord. *"Ye shall be witnesses unto Me" (Acts 1:8).*

CONCLUSION

Now that we have seen these six great truths in the life of Phebe, it is my prayer that they may be found in the lives of all the ladies who are a part of the Phebe Fellowship.

The Lord gave my husband a message on the life of Phebe, and as he thought on it he realized that these are truths that all Christian women need to embrace. The Lord reveals them so simply in Phebe's life.

Remember the great truth found in *John 8:32, "And ye shall know the truth, and the truth shall make you free."* It is truth that "makes" us new people. Truth transforms us. These six truths should transform us into Christians who become more Christ-like.

The Phebe Fellowship is a way of life. We should desire to have all six of these ingredients. We are what we are because of the truth we have been taught, and because of the people who have touched our lives.

The Apostle Paul said in *II Timothy 3:10*, *"But thou hast fully known my doctrine, manner of life, purpose, faith, longsuffering, charity, patience."* *"Doctrine"* is truth. Truth will change the way we live, our *"manner of life."* The way we live will change our *"purpose."* The truth taught in these lessons should change the way we live. The truth of Phebe Fellowship should become a way of life.

As a new Christian I had the privilege to be a part of the great Highland Park Baptist Church in Chattanooga, Tennessee, when Dr. Lee Roberson was pastor. Dr. and Mrs. Lee Roberson are two of the greatest Christians that I have ever known. I also had the privilege of spending one year with my dear sister-in-law, Evelyn Sexton, who is married to my husband's brother, Dr. Clarence Sexton. We were all members of Highland Park Baptist Church and served under the leadership of Dr. and Mrs. Roberson. Mrs. Roberson and Evelyn both typify what the Phebe Fellowship is all about.

As I reflect on my life, I realize that there were many women at Highland Park Baptist Church who had been touched and transformed by the life and ministry of Dr. Roberson. When I arrived in Chattanooga as a new Christian the ladies of that great church welcomed me and helped me to become someone the Lord could use. The truth that I learned in those years is the same truth that my husband and I have tried to put in the hearts and lives of the ladies to whom we have been privileged to minister. The truths that we now call the Phebe Fellowship are the same truths that had become a way of life for the ladies that helped me in my early years as a new Christian.

They loved me and welcomed me into their fellowship. They saw something in me that I did not see in myself. The ladies of that great church had such a loving fellowship. They accepted me where I was and treated me as an equal. It was as though they had been waiting on me and

I had been looking for them. They helped stir up a desire in my heart to become all that God wanted me to be. Through their lives and testimonies I saw what it meant to be **a sister** in the Lord. It had become a way of life for them.

These women brought me along with them. They taught me how to serve the Lord and have a heart for the Lord's work. Through their encouragement, I became an important part of the ministry, or at least they made me feel that way. I started by serving in the nursery. Then I sang in the choir. I helped with the children's ministry and started working on a bus route. Whenever I saw a need I was encouraged to serve the Lord in that area. I was taught the second great truth, to be **a servant of the church**.

Even though I had a long way to go, they accepted me where I was. When the time was right, they showed me the next step in my Christian life. I was encouraged to keep moving forward in my faith and walk. I was taught the third great truth, to be **set apart as becometh saints**. None of us have arrived. We must keep moving forward in our Christian lives. We need to keep taking the next step.

Then I was shown a bigger picture of God's work. For the first time in my life, I began to see missions and I understood that I needed to have a part in world evangelism. I became involved in personal soul winning. I was taught the fourth great truth, having a part in missions, and I understood what it meant to be **sent** to the mission field. As we have grown in the Lord, we have tried to have more of a part in missions. One of the blessings God gave me was allowing me to work as a secretary for a mission board.

The ladies who helped me as a new Christian also realized that if I were to continue to be faithful to the Lord, I would have to become a stronger Christian. They were aware of the battles that I would one day fight. They knew and understood the secret of being a five-star Christian.

They worked hard to strengthen me. I was taught the fifth great truth, the importance of **strengthening God's people**.

They taught me the sixth great truth of being **a personal soul winner**. We must all realize that we need to be faithful witnesses. The Lord will bring into our lives people with whom we can personally share the gospel. If we are not faithful witnesses, the people who come into our lives will probably not have a chance to be saved.

These six truths that I have been taught, and that we have worked so hard to teach others, will transform anyone's life. Let us continue to strengthen all six areas in each of our lives.

We need to ask the Lord to give us the power to become what Phebe had become. *John 1:12* says, *"But as many as received Him, to them gave He power to become…"* Remember, God created us for His pleasure and has designed a purpose for our lives. *Revelation 4:11* says, *"Thou art worthy, O Lord, to receive glory and honour and power: for Thou hast created all things, and for Thy pleasure they are and were created."*

A Christian Women's Ministry

BRINGING MEN TO CHRIST

For additional helpful publications,
and for Phebe Fellowship or Andrew Fellowship materials,
please visit:

www.fivestarchristianministries.com

Phebe Fellowship

A Christian Women's Ministry

Five Star
CHRISTIAN MINISTRIES

SCAN
ME